The Essence of

Aikido

Morihei Ueshiba

The Essence of

Spiritual Teachings of Morihei Ueshiba

Compiled by

John Stevens

KODANSHA INTERNATIONAL
Tokyo • New York • London

The calligraphy works *Aiki Ōkami* (P. 83) and *Takemusu Aiki* (P. 84) are
reprinted by permission of Seiseki Abe

Distributed in the United States by Kodansha America Inc., 114 Fifth
Avenue, New York, N.Y. 10011, and in the United Kingdom and
continental Europe by Kodansha Europe Ltd., 95 Aldwych, London
WC2B 4JF. Published by Kodansha International Ltd., 17–14 Otowa
1-chome, Bunkyo-ku, Tokyo 112, and Kodansha America Inc.

First edition, 1993
93 94 95 96 97 10 9 8 7 6 5 4 3 2 1

ISBN 4-7700-1727-8

Library of Congress Cataloging-in-Publication Data

Ueshiba Morihei, 1883–1969.
The essence of Aikidō : spiritual teachings of Morihei Ueshiba /
compiled and edited by John Stevens, under the direction of
Kisshōmaru Ueshiba.—1st ed.
p.   cm.
Translated from the Japanese.
Contents: 1. The universe of Aikidō 2. Songs of the path 3. Morihei's
calligraphic legacy 4. Misogi 5. The art of Aikidō.
ISBN 4-7700-1727-8
1. Aikido. I. Stevens, John, 1947–
II. Ueshiba, Kisshōmaru, 1921–
III. Title.
GV1114.35.U42 1993
796.8'154—dc20   93–34397
CIP

CONTENTS

Foreword

Expertly compiled and translated into English by Professor John Stevens, *The Essence of Aikidō* presents the spiritual teachings of Morihei Ueshiba, the founder of Aikidō.

The discipline of Aikidō, based on the unity of body and mind, is a search for a higher state of consciousness through sincere practice; reliance on words and letters alone will never suffice. Furthermore, in all of the traditional "Ways" of the East, it is important to walk that Path continually, it being a grave error to be satisfied with one's attainments.

In this context, the contents of *The Essence of Aikidō* are most appropriate. The compiler John Stevens is an enthusiastic, long-time practitioner of Aikidō and he presents the challenging material in light of his own understanding and first-hand experiences. Since each practitioner of Aikidō must develop his or her own perception of Morihei's teachings, as expressed in his writings, calligraphy, and poems, *The Essence of Aikidō* will be an invaluable resource.

Recently the number of people throughout the world diligently practicing Aikidō while seeking to grasp the spirit of the founder's teachings has greatly increased, and this makes me truly happy. It is my sincere hope that each student of Aikidō will establish his or her own path—slowly and correctly, step-by-step—through rigorous practice.

Finally, Professor Stevens deserves special praise for his devotion to Aikidō and I congratulate him on completing this worthwhile project.

Kisshōmaru Ueshiba
Aikidō Dōshū

Preface

Morihei Ueshiba's spiritual teachings collected in *The Essence of Aikidō* form the companion volume to *Budō: Teachings of the Founder of Aikidō*. The first chapter, "The Universe of Aikidō," and the fourth chapter, "Misogi: Purification of Body and Mind," are based on material from *Aiki Shinzui*, a collection of transcripts of Morihei's talks.

In the second chapter, "Songs of the Path," a number of Morihei's didactic poems are presented—originally such poems were recited to a special rhythm, hence their designation as "songs." Songs of the Path by a master are said to possess twelve levels of meaning and are traditionally circulated without written commentary. However, I felt it necessary to annotate those poems containing unusually difficult terminology and obscure references. The translations of the songs are fairly literal, but my renderings are always based on the "spirit rather than the letter." The Japanese originals with romanization are provided for those who wish to tackle Morihei's verse directly. In this book I have generally translated 道 *dō* (*michi*) as "Path" rather than "Way." In the present text, "Path" refers to a particular discipline, such as Aikidō, that follows a certain route; "Way" involves a broader spectrum of universal principles. Aikidō is, of course, both a Path and a Way, so this distinction may appear somewhat arbitrary, but I ask the indulgence of my readers.

The third chapter, "Morihei's Calligraphic Legacy," presents examples of Morihei's brushwork from the collection of the Ueshiba family.

The book concludes with "The Art of Aikidō," comprising over two hundred illustrations of Morihei performing the techniques. Covering the entire range of Morihei's Aikidō, the photos include previously unpublished shots from the 1936 Noma Dōjō series, out-takes from Morihei's 1938 book *Budō*, shots taken outdoors in Wakayama in 1968, and various other shots of Morihei in action in his final years.

John Stevens

PART
I

The Universe of Aikidō

Morihei Ueshiba insisted that "Aikidō is the study of the spirit." His own life was one long spiritual quest, an intense longing for the Divine, and his search for the deeper truths of religion and philosophy never ceased. Morihei pored over sacred texts, meditated on the mysteries of existence, prayed constantly to the gods, forged his body ceaselessly, and was ultimately transformed by the most profound visions.

Aikidō was revealed to Morihei as an all-embracing path, an eclectic system containing elements of esoteric Shintō, Tantric Buddhism, Taoism, Confucianism, and even Christianity. He once said:

> The Aikidō I practice has room for each of the world's eight million gods and I cooperate with each one of them. The Great Spirit of Aiki enjoins all that is Divine and enlightened in every land. Unite yourself to the Divine, and you will be able to perceive gods wherever you are.

Like most masters, Morihei conveyed his teachings through image, symbol, and allegory. His talks could be bewilderingly complex, delivered in a kind of secret "twilight language" that demanded one's utmost attention.

Morihei's message was set forth in terms of 言霊 *kototama*, "language of the spirit." *Koto* means "word, language, speech"; *tama* signifies "spirit or soul." (The combination of the two characters is usually pronounced *kotodama*, but Morihei's preference was *kototama*.) Morihei maintained that the seed-sounds of *kototama* "direct and harmonize all things in the world, resulting in the unification of heaven, earth, gods, and humankind."

Seers and sages of many traditional cultures taught that the universe was "sung" into existence by the vibration of sacred sounds. These word-souls activate all forms of life and then sustain creation by continually crystallizing into function and structure (*koto* also means "action" and "object"). The concept of *kototama* is quite similar to the notion of

Logos—"the Word"—as expressed in the opening line of the Gospel of St. John in the New Testament, which may be paraphrased as follows:

> In the beginning was the Word and the Word was with God, and the Word was God…All things came into being through the Word and without it not one thing was made. What came into being was Life, the Life which was the Light of humankind.

Morihei, in fact, liked to use this quotation when explaining *kototama* to Westerners. In Japanese translation, the character 道 ("way," "path") was used to represent the concept of *Logos*. Just as the Word was "made

Morihei reciting a prayer in front of the Aiki Shrine in Iwama.

flesh, and dwelt among us...full of grace and truth" (John 1:14), Mori-hei's mastery of *kototama* allowed him to reestablish the true meaning and function of things. In short, *kototama* is a code based on the primary and universal Word—it is the language of poetry, prayer, incantation, mythology, and philosophy as well as the animating resonance of music.

Morihei's *kototama* theory derived from his experiences with Shingon ("True Word") Buddhism, from Ōmoto-kyō mysticism, and from his study of the Shintō scriptures *Kojiki* and *Nihon shoki,* but he eventually developed his own spiritual language to express the rich texture of Aikidō. Although Morihei's presentation of *kototama* philosophy is rooted in a particular tradition and milieu, it relates universal principles that are valid for any time or place. Once the essence of Morihei's *kototama* system is understood, it can be translated into any idiom.

Aikidō Cosmology

Aikidō has its own cosmology. When asked "What is Aikidō?" Morihei would on occasion draw a diagram in response, and in this section several of his Aikidō mandalas will be discussed.

The first mandala (Fig. 1) is entitled, across the top from right to left, 天之武産合氣業 *Ame no Takemusu Aiki Waza*, "The Functioning of Heaven's *Takemusu Aiki*." *Ame*, "heaven," is comprised of the *kototama* ア A, "self," and メ ME, "rotation," indicating the cosmos to be "that which circulates within and all about us." *Takemusu Aiki* will be explained in detail later, but here it means "Valorous Force of Procreation and Harmony." *Waza*, translated in this case as "functioning," is also the term for "technique."

Written down the left side of the mandala at the top is 合氣之母 *Aiki no ama (haha)*, "Mother of Aiki," and, at the bottom, 常盛謹書 *Tsunemori kinsho*, "Respectfully brushed by Tsunemori." (Tsunemori, "Always Abundant," was one of Morihei's pen names.)

Down the right side we find on the inside ホノサワケ（中津国）*Honosawake (Nakatsu-kuni)*. *Honosawake* is one of the names given to the first island of the Japanese archipelago to be created. The term means "Rice-Ear-True-Youth," a symbol of fertility and growth. Morihei interpreted 淡道之穂之狭別 *Ahaji-no-honosawake* (the full name of the island) as representing the physical manifestation of universal spiritual principles. In this mandala, Morihei also equates the phrase with *Nakatsu-kuni*, "Land in the Middle Ocean," signifying the center of our own world.

On the outside is written 天の村雲九鬼さむはら龍王之御道 *Ame-no-murakumo-kuki-samuhara Ryūō no godō*. This means "Honored Path of [the Guardian Deity] *Ame-no-murakumo-kuki-samuhara Ryūō*." As will be explained later, Morihei considered himself to be an incarnation of this Dragon King, and in this mandala Morihei declares his single-minded intent to make known the sacred mission of Aikidō while being inspired and guided by that deity.

At the heart of the mandala is a circle, and in its center a dot superimposed by the symbol ス SU, the seed-sound of the universe. SU is the *kototama* of creation, the pure vibration out of which all things emanate. From this incomprehensibly dense point steam, smoke, and mist pour forth in a nebulous sphere while the *kototama* ウ U spirals forth, giving birth to the phenomenal world as it rotates in an ウ ー ウ ー ウ ー ユ ー ム

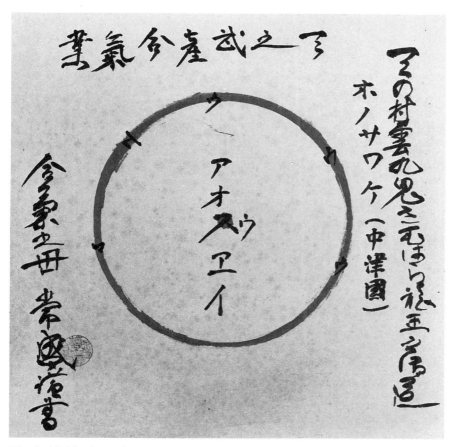

Fig. 1 Aikidō Cosmology

U–U–U–YU–MU pattern. According to *kototama* theory U = procreation; YU = harmonization of fire and water; MU = physical birth. In Shintō mythology, SU is identified with 天御中主神 *Ame-no-minaka-nushi-no-kami*, "Lord Deity of Heaven's Center." The U–U–U–YU–MU progression evolves into two primordial generative forces: 高御産巣日神 *Takami-musubi-no-kami*, "High August Growth Deity," and 神御産巣日神 *Kami-musubi-no-kami*, "Divine August Growth Deity." Allegorically, *Ame-no-minaka-nushi-no-kami* is the fulcral point of creation, while *Takami-musubi-no-kami* and *Kami-no-musubi-no-kami* are the two poles of centripetal and centrifugal force which hold things together. *Takami-musubi-no-kami* expands, swells, exhales, and diversifies; it is most active in Spring and Summer. *Kami-no-musubi-no-kami* contracts, absorbs, inhales, and unifies; it is most active in Autumn and Winter.

Simultaneously SU expands vertically into the kototama アーオーウーエーイ A–O–U–E–I. (These *kototama* are strikingly similar to the "simple" vowels that form the core of most of the world's languages; such vowels are the vibrant sounds that bring speech to life when combined with the more inert consonants.)

Morihei explained the special qualities of each of these *kototama* as follows:

A [pronounced like the English "ah"] signifies "creating something from nothing," "first among all sounds," "the sustainer of life," and "Mother Nature." A is associated with 国之常立神 *Kuni-no-tokotachi-no-kami*, "Earth Eternal Standing Deity." When the mouth is opened wide and the breath is expelled from the bottom of the throat, the sound A is made. The elongated pronunciation of A naturally leads to the sound O.

O ["o" as in "rose"] signifies "arising," "nobility," "exalted," and "that which links heaven and earth." O is associated with 豊雲野神 *Toyokumonu-no-kami*, "Abundant Clouds Field Deity." When the tongue comes to rest naturally in the mouth, the sound U occurs.

U ["u" as in "true"] signifies "floating up," "movement," "birth," "darkness," and "the principle that holds space together through cosmic breath." U is associated with 宇比地爾神 *Uhijini-no-kami*, "Floating Mud Deity." When strongly pronounced to the limit, U returns again to SU. SU, the sister deity of U, is associated with 須比智爾神 *Suhijini-no-kami*, "Sinking Sand Deity." If the tongue is extended and slightly curved when U is pronounced in the lower part of the mouth the sound E is naturally formed.

E ["e" as in "grey"] signifies the "placenta of heaven and earth," "limbs," and "branches." Since E becomes レ RE when the tongue is moved to the roof of the mouth, E is associated with 角杙神 *Tsunuguhi-no-kami*, "Male Root Deity," and 生杙神 *Ikuguhi-no-kami*, "Female Root Deity." The pronunciation of E naturally tapers off into the sound I.

I ["i" as in "machine"] signifies "outbreath," "animation," and "life force." When pronounced strongly I naturally becomes ギ GI, the *kototama* that defines the boundaries of existence. Therefore, I is associated with 意富斗能地神 *Ootonoji-no-kami*, "Great Male Joining Deity," and GI is associated with 大斗乃 弁神 *Ootonobe-no-kami*, "Great Female Joining Deity."

These five *kototama* are the great vowels that constitute the Word of Creation. All together they are associated with 面足神 *Omodaru-no-kami*, "Male Perfect Form Deity" and 阿夜可志古 泥神 *Ayakashikone-no-kami*, "Female Most Awesome Deity."

In more direct terms, these five *kototama* and their associated deities symbolize the process of creation:

A (Earth Eternal Standing Deity) represents the spark of material creation.

O (Abundant Clouds Field Deity) represents the moist, steamy, and luxuriant "cosmic broth" from which life sprang.

U (Floating Mud Deity–Sinking Sand Deity) represents the process of half-liquid, half-solid sedimentation.

E (Male Root Deity–Female Root Deity) represents the germination of biological life.

I (Great Male Joining Deity–Great Female Joining Deity) represents bisexual differentiation.

A–O–U–E–I (Male Perfect Form Deity–Female Most Awesome Deity) represent the concluding stages of creation where mutual perception and awareness occur. (These five seed-sounds spread out, up and down, right and left, and then expand into a circle that vivifies all seventy-five *kototama* of the Japanese language.)

When the process described above is complete, the deities 伊耶
那岐 *Izanagi*, "He-Who-Invites" and 伊耶那美 *Izanami*, "She-
Who-Invites" appear in human form. The pair eventually created, through sexual interaction, the islands of Japan beginning
with *Honosawake*.

(It is interesting to note that this scheme of creation—which largely
parallels modern scientific thinking—maintains that everything is copro-
duced by male-female union rather than following the fiat of a patriar-
chal god. In Aikidō, the world is not governed by a celestial lawgiver, but
rather depends on the harmonious cooperation of all beings acting in
accordance with their spontaneous and free inner natures.)

When Morihei meditated on and pronounced these *kototama*, he said,
"The gods performing those functions gather around me." He sub-
merged himself in the very act of creation, from the most subtle to the
most concrete. (The sequence used for the verbalization of these *kototama*
is A → O → U → E → I and then back to A, usually repeating the cycle
a number of times.)

On occasion Morihei utilized the *kototama* ターカーアーマーハーラ
（高天原） TA–KA–A–MA–HA–RA, "High Heavenly Plain," exempli-
fying, on the cosmic level, "original void" and, on a personal level, "a
pure state of mind." Morihei explained the function of these six *kototama*
as:

TA = the creative tension—between water and fire, *yin* and
yang, hidden and manifest, stillness and motion, life and
death—that establishes existence

KA = the creative tension that sustains existence

A = the full extension of the physical universe

MA = the microscopic jewels (atoms) that support that extension

HA = the vital energy that animates the world

RA = the circulation and distribution of those energy-waves

Morihei compared the practice of *kototama* to the act of *Izanagi* and *Izanami* standing on the 天の浮橋 *Ame-no-ukihashi*, "The Floating Bridge of Heaven," to create the world in which we dwell. ア A = self, メ ME = circulate, ウ キ U-KI = vertical water element, and ハ シ HA-SHI = horizontal fire element. In other words, the Floating Bridge of Heaven lies at the center of the space-time continuum where fire and water intersect. It is the link between Heaven and Earth, the Divine and Humankind, and it is the place where each person must stand to find his or her true self.

> The heart of a human being is no different from the soul of heaven and earth. In your practice always keep your mind on the interaction of heaven and earth, water and fire, *yin* and *yang*.

In this way, Morihei would visualize himself standing on the Floating Bridge of Heaven, form a cross with his fan or the *jō,* and then bring forth the *kototama* O, vocalized as an extended note. Morihei said of all these *kototama* practices:

> Let those *kototama* percolate inside of you, firing the blood until your entire body is congealed into a *kototama*. Imagine yourself expanding into a large circle, voice the *kototama*, and then sense the universe gathering within. This practice creates light [wisdom], heat [compassion], and energy [true strength].

Kototama provided Morihei with the substance and sustenance of Aikidō.

This mandala also has practical application, elucidated by Morihei in the following manner:

> *Ame-no-minaka-nushi-no-kami*, the point SU of creation, is none other than one's own spiritual and physical center located in the area around the navel. This is the golden cauldron where the "blood boils" and where *kototama* spiral forth. One should always be centered there during the practice of Aikidō.

Regarding the prototypes *Izanami* and *Izanagi*, Morihei said:

> *Izanami* is the female, receptive element associated with water, centrifugal force, and the right side of things; *Izanagi* is the male, active element associated with fire, centripetal force, and the left side of things. Left is activation, the key element of entering, and the source of unlimited variations; right is reception, the key element of control, directing and commanding *ki*. The left shields, the right strengthens.

Morihei taught that the movements of Aikidō must incorporate and unify these two components—and for this reason the techniques are always practiced from both sides of the body: "Functioning harmoniously, right and left give birth to all techniques. The left hand confronts life and death directly while the right controls it."

The second mandala (Fig. 2) depicts the cosmic patterns of 布斗麻邇 *futomani*. On one level, *futomani* is an ancient system of divination involving the interpretation of cracks appearing on the shoulder-blade bone of a stag after being heated in a fire. The cracks were read by Shintō soothsayers, and the patterns that appeared on the bone are held to be the basis of the Japanese *kana* syllabary, the visual representations of *kototama*. On a deeper level, *futomani*—the balance of motion and stillness, the transmutation of body and soul—was thought to communicate the universal code of natural intelligence, an arrangement of root concepts and archetypes that imparted all wisdom to those who grasped its essence.

Thus, Morihei states in the long inscription on the left side of the mandala: 比形ハ布斗麻邇御霊ヨリ割別タル水火ノ形ナリ之ヲ以テ天地ノ気ヲ知ルコトヲ得（ト相布斗麻邇御灵知天地人之初発但シ布斗麻邇ニ占ナエテトハウノ御活力用）"These patterns depict the individual functions branching off from the Sacred Spirit of *futomani*, the pattern of water and fire. This scheme enables one to attain knowledge of the *ki* of heaven and earth. (It also allows one to divine the origins of heaven, earth, and humankind—such *futomani* divination is the active functioning of the [*kototama*] U.)"

Along the right side at the top, Morihei has entitled the mandala 武産合気 *Takemusu Aiki* and added his signature at the bottom, 常盛 *Tsunemori*. In smaller characters alongside *Takemusu Aiki* it says

イキ共に調ヒテ *I-ki tomo ni totonoite*, "I-KI should be in balance," refer-
ring to the two diagrams.

The simple diagram at the top is the point of creation. The outer circle
is the Mother (water) and the dot in the center is Father (fire). From
there, I (the out-breath symbolized by the eight-spoked circle ⊛) rises
and KI (the in-breath represented by the eight-triangle square ⊠)
descends. When the two elements I and KI are balanced we have the sus-
taining force of physical existence.

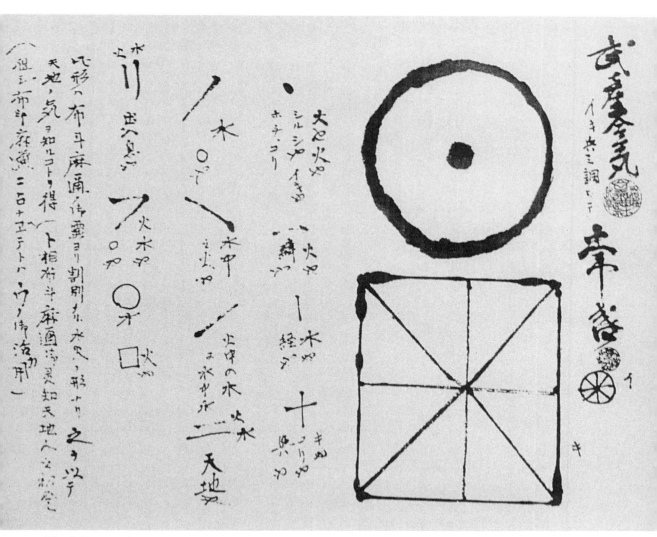

Fig. 2 *Futomani*

The rest of the mandala explains the symbolism of other patterns of nature:

❟	大也火也 シルシ也イキ也 ポチ、コリ	Vastness, Fire, Dot, Life, Point, Congealed Essence
一	火也緯也	Fire, Woof of Existence
丨	水也経也	Water, Warp of Existence
十	キ也コリ也 興也	*Ki*, Concreteness, Integration
〰	水○也	Water, Roundness
〱	水中之火也	Fire Within Water
丿	火中の水 又水中水	Water Within Fire, Water Within Water
二	火 水 天地也	(top line) Fire (bottom line) Water (together) Heaven-Earth
火 水 リ	火　水	(left) Fire　　(right) Water
	出入息也	Out- / In-breath
フ	火水也○也	Fire-Water, Roundness
○	水	Water
口	火也	Fire

⊙ is a universal symbol for the Source. The circle stands for the macrocosm (water) while the axial point represents the microcosm (fire). In Indian philosophy, this symbol is called *bindu* (seed), and in Western thought it is termed *sol* (golden sun) by alchemists and *theos* (god) by theologians. In Aikidō cosmology, it is the ground of being from which all things are born. The Japanese term for birth is ウム U-MU, consisting of the *kototama* 有 U, "Being" and 無 MU, "Nothingness." That is, life springs forth when Form and Emptiness are in perfect balance. Morihei also referred to this state as 真空 *shinkū*, "True Emptiness." "Stand in true emptiness," Morihei taught, "And you will transcend life and death. This is the essence of Aikidō."

The fundamental factor of life is I-KI, "Breath." The *kototama* U spirals forth from the seed-sound SU, fashioning the out-breath and the in-breath of life. The out-breath is circular ⊕ in the shape of the water element, and it is the basis of the Breath of Heaven; the in-breath is square ⊠ in the shape of the fire element, and is the basis of the Breath of Earth, settling deep within the body. Conversely, the Breath of Heaven is the breath of the sun, moon, and stars; the Breath of Earth is the breath of the ebb and flow of the tide. When the Breath of Heaven and the Breath of Earth are fully integrated we have Human Breath, the wellspring of our life. Breath provides us with the means for uttering the *kototama*, and breath-power enables us to execute all the techniques of Aikidō:

> Everything in heaven and earth breathes. Breath is the thread that ties creation together. When the myriad variations in universal breath can be sensed, the individual techniques of Aikidō are born.

Morihei often spoke of the 阿吽 A-UN breath. A-UN is the Japanese pronunciation of the Sanskrit AUM (OM), the sum of all sounds, the actualization of cosmic breath involving the creation, integration, and completion of all things. (In the West, the equivalent of OM is ALPHA-OMEGA.) OM has the connotation of "reverence, agreement, acceptance," and represents the affirmation of life. Morihei taught:

> Rise early in the morning to greet the sun. Breathe in and let yourself soar to the ends of the universe; breathe out and bring

the cosmos back inside. Next breathe up all the fecundity and vibrancy of the earth. Finally, blend the Breath of Earth with that of your own, becoming the Breath of Life itself. Your body and mind will be gladdened, depression and heartache will dissipate, and you will be filled with gratitude.

水火 I-KI is also read "Water-Fire," the Japanese version of the Chinese 陰陽 *yin-yang* cosmology. (Water and fire are also the two basic components of Western alchemy.) The water-fire balance is often formulated in this manner:

WATER	FIRE
feminine	masculine
receptive	active
stillness	motion
hidden	manifest
shade	light
eros	logos
growing	sowing
▽ *yoni*	△ *linga*
womb	heart
right	left
white tiger	azure dragon
earth	heaven
moon	sun

As shown in the *futomani* chart, the interaction—woof and warp—of these two aggregates and their components leads to creation. When reversed as 火水 Fire-Water, the characters are read *kami*, "Divine."

Water-Fire is activated by 気 *ki*, the energy that propels the universe and the cohesive force that holds things together. Everything must be endowed with energy before it can assume material form: plants have *ki* + sentience, animals have *ki* + sentience + intelligence, and human beings have *ki* + sentience + intelligence + a conscience.

Morihei constantly urged his disciples to "link yourself to the *ki* of true emptiness":

> There are two types of *ki*: ordinary *ki* and true *ki*. Ordinary *ki* is coarse and heavy; true *ki* is light and versatile. In order to perform well, you have to liberate yourself from ordinary *ki* and permeate your organs with true *ki*. Strength resides where one's *ki* is concentrated and stable; confusion and maliciousness reign where *ki* stagnates.

The source of *ki* in the body is the 気海丹田 *kikai tanden*, "*ki*-ocean-cinnabar-field." This chakra is located in the area around one's navel, the center of the body's gravity, where the alchemical furnace of *kototama* is found.

Regarding the order of things, Morihei often spoke of 魂魄 *kon-haku*. The concept of *kon* (conscious soul) and *haku* (corporeal soul) is very similar to the English notion of a person's "higher" and "lower" (or base) nature. *Kon* represents the higher nature of a human being: intelligence, conscience, spiritual sensitivity, and divine intuition; *haku* is the restless seat of the emotions: joy, anger, sorrow, fear, love, hate, and desire. *Kon* is the element of the human soul that "ascends" after death; *haku* is the element that "descends" to earth and is buried with the body.

An admixture of *kon* and *haku* are necessary for human existence—pure spirit cannot function in this world—but Morihei instructed his students to foster the *kon* aspect of the soul. "Vitalize, animate, and nourish the *kon* aspect of your soul, and you will naturally become more spiritual."

Morihei felt that all the martial arts heretofore were based primarily on the *haku* factor; Aikidō, on the other hand, is centered on the *kon* element. Aikidō is a spiritual, rather than a technical, art:

> Your heart is full of fertile seeds, waiting to sprout. Just as a lotus flower springs from the mire to bloom splendidly, the interaction of the Breath of Heaven and the Breath of Earth, and the subtle functioning of fire and water cause the flower of the spirit to bloom in this world of materialism.

The next mandala (Fig. 3) deals with two essential components of Morihei's philosophy: *Takemusu Aiki* and *Masakatsu-Agatsu-Katsuhayabi*. In the center space there is 天の○ *Ame no maru*, the empty circle of Heaven. Morihei once remarked, "The essence of Aikidō is zero." To the right in the first line is 正勝吾勝 *Masakatsu-Agatsu*, in the second 天の武産 ㊥ 合氣 *Ame-no-Takemusu SU Aiki*, and in the third 勝速日 *Katsuhayabi*.

Masakatsu-Agatsu-Katsuhayabi (variously pronounced *Masakatsu-Akatsu-Kachihayahi* or *Masakatsu-Warekatsu-Kachihayabi*) is part of the name of a Shintō deity brought into being by the gods *Susano-o* and *Amaterasu*. It is also a phrase from a secret chant used for centuries by mountain ascetics and samurai saints. On certain evenings, these practitioners would fix their gaze on the moon and pronounce this mantra:

SU-U-KU KA-MI SA-MU-HA-RA
MA-SA-KA-TSU WA-RE-KA-TSU KA-CHI-HA-YA-BI

It may be interpreted as meaning:

Outpouring-Creation-Space-Divine-Integration
True Victory is Self-Victory, Day of Swift Victory!

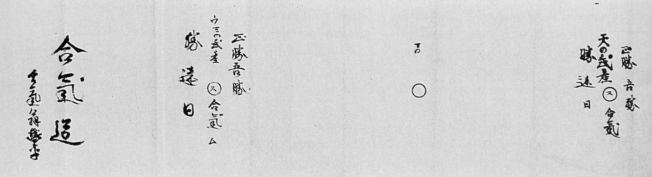

Fig. 3 *Masakatsu-Agatsu-Katsuhayabi*

In order to master the mysteries of *Budō*, one must return to the source of things and unite oneself with the Divine; the only way to be invincible is to overcome one's base passions, to defeat the mind of contention within, and to achieve complete clarity of mind. Then one can anticipate any attack and escape unharmed.

Morihei took *Masakatsu-Agatsu-Katsuhayabi* as his motto and explained it like this:

> The heart of Aikidō is: True Victory is Self-Victory, Day of Swift Victory! "True Victory" means unflinching courage; "Self-Victory" symbolizes unflagging effort; and "Day of Swift Victory" represents the glorious moment of triumph in the here and now. Aikidō is free of set forms, so it responds immediately to any contingency, which thus assures us of the true victory; it is invincible because it contends with nothing. Rely on "True Victory is Self-Victory, Day of Swift Victory" and you will be able to integrate the inner and outer factors of practice, clear your path of obstacles, and cleanse your senses.

Morihei further stated:

> If all you think about is winning you will in fact lose everything. Know that both you and your oppponents are treading the same path. Envelop adversaries with love, entrust yourself to the natural flow of things, unify *ki*, body, and mind, and efface the boundary between self and other. This opens unlimited possibilities. Those who are enlightened to these principles are always victorious. Winning without contending is true victory, a victory over oneself, a victory swift and sure. Victory is to harmonize self and other, to link yourself to the Divine, to yoke yourself to Divine Love, to become the universe itself.

Morihei described the esoteric significance of *Masakatsu-Agatsu-Katsuhayabi* in the following way:

> *Masakatsu* represents the masculine fire element of the left; *Agatsu* stands for the feminine water element of the right; *Katsuhayabi* is the perfect combination of both that empowers the techniques. If the techniques are true like this, victory will be directly at hand.

Take, the first element of *Takemusu*, is also pronounced *bu*. The primary meaning is "martial," but the Chinese character for *bu* literally means "putting a stop to contending spears," that is to say, "to quell disturbances and keep the peace." Morihei taught that *take/bu* embodied the valor, bravery, wisdom, and compassion of the Divine, and that it is a dynamic, vigorous force that protects and nourishes all things.

> *Take/bu* is Divine. It is a path established by the gods grounded in truth, goodness, and beauty. *Take/bu* is righteousness. It makes us strong and heroic, and it allows us to manifest courage, wisdom, love, and empathy. *Take/bu* is a mirror that reveals all things and exposes evil.

Musu means "birth," "becoming," "generation," "creative power," "fecundate" as well as "ferment," "brew," and "percolate." It is the abbreviation of 産日 *musubi* (*bi* signifies the "wondrous light" of the vital force, much like "And God saw that light was good" of Genesis 1:4). *Musubi* links all things together in an interconnected web, a web that extends without beginning or end. *Musubi* "ties the knot" and is a symbol of marriage and coproduction.

Musubi transcends the distinction between self and other and thus leads to the wholeness of *Aiki*, the "harmonious force" that reconciles and blends opposites, and calms all discord. *Musubi/Aiki* is a dialectical process that binds together such elements as the following in a seamless unity:

fire	water
male	female
in-breath	out-breath
front	back
extension	contraction
expansion	absorption
diversity	unity

Aiki also connotes "mutual assistance," and Morihei further equated *Aiki* with 愛気 *aiki*, "the purest manifestation of love."

Takemusu Aiki is the "Valorous Procreative Force of Harmony," irrepressibly life-generating, fully integrated, totally free, and capable of unlimited transformations.

On the left of the diagram (Fig. 3) on the first line is written: 正勝吾勝 *Masakatsu-Agatsu*; on the second line ウ天の武産㊄合氣ム *U Ame no*

Takemusu SU Aiki MU; and on the third line 勝速日 *Katsuhayabi.* The addition of U-MU, "birth," emphasizes the divine productivity and wholeness of *Takemusu Aiki.*

The mandala ends with the affirmation 合氣道 Aikidō. Morihei's "Way of Harmony" is a path that directs us toward truth, goodness, and beauty; it reflects the unlimited, absolute nature of the universe and the ultimate grand design of creation. Morihei said this about the "Way":

> The Way is like the veins that circulate blood through our bodies, following the natural flow of the life force. If you are separated in the slightest from that Divine essence, you are far off the path.

In a triumphant finale, the mandala is signed 合氣翁盛平 *Aiki Ō Morihei* "Morihei, the Old Fellow of Aiki." The founder declares here that Aikidō is not an abstraction; it was Morihei's own body and soul and it can live too in each and everyone of us.

Morihei often used the symbolism of triangle, circle, and square (Fig. 4) to illustrate the principle of 一霊四魂三元八力 *ichirei-shikon-sangen-*

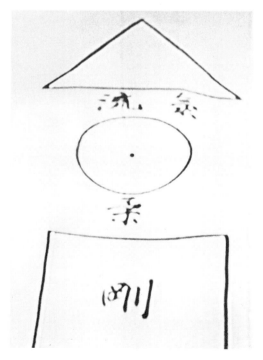

Fig. 4 Triangle, Circle, Square from a chart drawn by Morihei.

hachiriki, "One-Spirit, Four-Souls, Three-Fundamentals, and Eight-Powers," a framework that Morihei believed was present in every religious cosmology.

One Spirit

一霊 "One-Spirit" is the single source of creation, identified in Aikidō as the seed *kototama* SU, which spiraled into KA-MI, Fire and Water, thus forming all other components of existence. The One Spirit permeates the cosmos.

The Four Souls

奇霊 *kushi-mitama* is the intelligent, profound, mysterious, and sensitive aspect of the human soul. It is the source of wisdom, clarity, and virtue. *Kushi-mitama* is associated with Heaven and the principle of centralization.

荒霊 *ara-mitama*, is the rough, wild, and fierce aspect of human nature. It is the source of courage, valor, and progress and, if properly channeled, it is an intelligent, powerful constructive force. *Ara-mitama* is associated with Fire and the principle of industry. (When Morihei was displeased with something, his *ara-mitama* manifested itself as explosive anger. Anyone scolded by Morihei never forgot it.)

和霊 *nigi-mitama* is the gentle, peaceful, and mild aspect of the human soul that seeks harmony and peace, and is the source of empathy, trust, and respect. *Nigi-mitama* is associated with Water and the principle of consolidation.

幸霊 *sachi-mitama* is the optimistic, bright, and flourishing aspect of the human soul that bestows the blessings of happiness, and is the source of love and compassion. *Sachi-mitama* is associated with Earth and the principle of differentiation.

The Three Fundamentals

△ represents 生霊 *iku-musubi* (also pronounced *iku-tama*), "Vivifying Fundamental," the *ki*-flow dimension. It symbolizes initiative, the animal realm, and *Masakatsu*. Technically, the triangle is the key to "entering."

○ represents 足霊 *taru-musubi* (*taru-tama*), "Completing Fundamental," the liquid dimension. It symbolizes unification, the vegetable realm, and *Agatsu*. Technically, the circle is the key to "blending."

□ represents 玉留霊 *tamatsume-musubi* (*tamatsume-tama*), "Fulfilling Fundamental," the solid dimension. It symbolizes form, the mineral realm, and *Katsuhayabi*. Technically, the square is the key to "control."

The Eight Powers

Movement	Calm
Release	Solidification
Retraction	Extension
Unification	Division

The next mandala (Fig. 5) in this section is a portrait of Morihei. The inscription—"Aikidō is all I am"—reveals exactly how Morihei viewed himself.

The first line on the right is 速武産大神 *Haya-Takemusu-Ōkami*, "Swift Valorous Creative Great Spirit." This is the universal oversoul out of which proceeds the particular incarnation on line two, 天の村雲九鬼さむはら龍王 *Ame-no-murakumo-kuki-samuhara Ryūō*. Morihei related that on December 14, 1940, the messenger *Saruta-hiko*—a god of ethics who leads people along the path of virtue—appeared to him and announced that *Ame-no-murakumo-kuki-samuhara Ryūō* would thereafter take possession of his soul. (The shock of this event was so great that Morihei was very ill for nearly a year after.)

Morihei explained the esoteric significance of the title of his incarnation in this fashion:

天の村雲 *Ame-no-murakumo*, "Billowing clouds of Heaven" = universal energy and all pervasive breath.
九鬼 *Kuki*, "Nine Fierce Spirits" (and the name of an ancient system of esoteric Shintō that Morihei studied deeply) = the physical realm of time, space, and continuity, "the double-edged sword of heaven and earth."

Fig. 5 "Aikidō is all I am"

Detail of Morihei's calligraphy in Fig. 5

さむはら *samuhara* "Cold Plain" = set aright, put in tune, proper formulation, purification.

龍王 *Ryūō* "Dragon King" = dynamic power that transmutes and controls the forces of nature.

In short, *Ame-no-murakumo-kuki-samuhara Ryūō* is a "Divine Agency Capable of Eradicating All Evil and Pacifying the World," a symbol of the world's highest virtue.

The third line is 勝速日降下 *Katsuhayabi koka*, "Day of Swift Victory has descended!" Morihei, divinely inspired, has made Aikidō accessible to all. The last line is an exuberant declaration: 合氣常盛 *Aiki Tsunemori*, "Tsunemori of Aiki!"

Morihei commissioned an artist named Jō-ō to paint him as *Ame-no-murakumo-kuki-samuhara Ryūō* (Fig. 6). The artist couldn't come up with a good image at first, so he meditated on the subject of Morihei/*Ame-no-murakumo-samuhara Ryūō* for several days and then created the painting all at once in an inspired burst of activity. Transformed into the soaring Dragon King, Morihei is portrayed amid swirling clouds of energy, his gaze firmly set on the Great Way of Aiki.

Fig. 6 Morihei depicted in the painting as a Dragon King. In front of the portrait sits Morihei's son, Kisshōmaru Ueshiba.

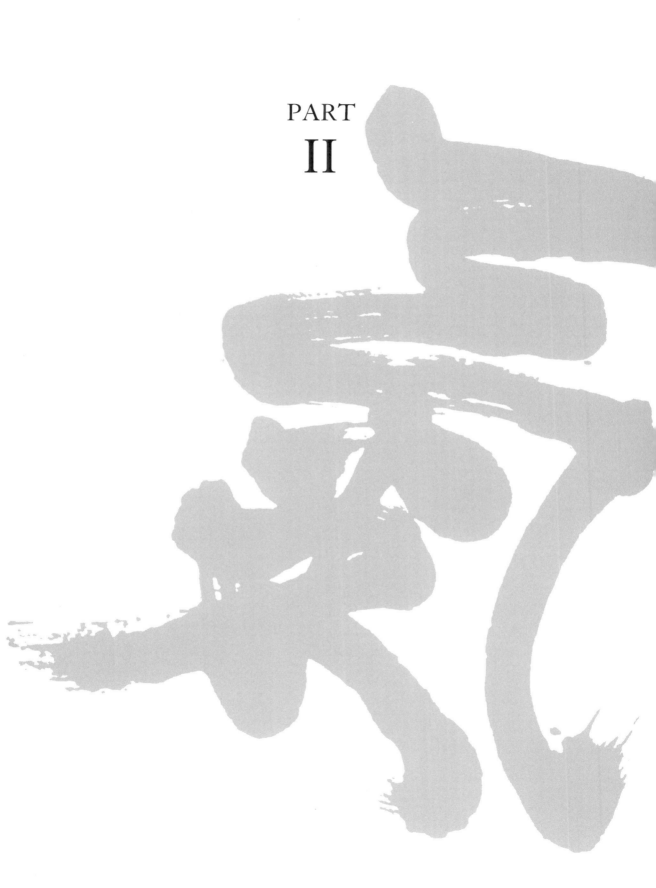

PART
II

SONGS OF THE PATH

Like many Japanese masters, Morihei employed 道歌 *dōka*, "Songs of the Path," to present his teachings. *Dōka* are poems with deep spiritual meaning arranged in the 5-7-5-7-7 syllable pattern of traditional Japanese 和歌 *waka* verse.

Such poetry can be a powerful *kototama*, and the first *waka* was said to be an incantation chanted by the goddess *Waka-Hime* to rid a rice paddy of a horde of locusts. (Incidentally, this act was said to have occurred in an area that was later called Wakayama—Morihei's birthplace.) Once the plague was lifted the rice plants were able to sprout again; thus one meaning of *waka* is to "enliven," and *dōka* are meant to be vehicles that convey a master's teaching in a fresh and vibrant manner.

One edition of Morihei's *dōka* contained this preface:

> Those who train in Aikidō must never forget that the teaching has to be forged in one's very body. Always keep in mind the Divine workings of creation, from beginning to end, and ceaselessly learn from the gods. Make the entire universe your *dōjō*. This is the great meaning of *Budō*.

(1) よろずすじ　　　　*Yorozu suji*
　　　限り知られぬ　　　*kagiri shirarenu*
　　　合気道　　　　　　*aikidō*
　　　世を開くべく　　　*yo o hiraku beku*
　　　人の身魂に　　　　*hito no mitama ni*

> Multifaceted,
> not knowing any boundaries,
> Aikidō—
> open it to the world,
> manifest it in everyone's body and soul!

(2)   大宇宙   *Dai uchū*
       合気の道は   *aiki no michi wa*
       もろ人の   *morobito no*
       光となりて   *hikari to narite*
       世をば開かん   *yo oba hirakan*

       The great universal
       Path of Aiki
       illuminates
       all people,
       opening the world [to the Truth].

(3)   合気にて   *Aiki nite*
       よろず力を   *yorozu chikara o*
       働かし   *hatarakashi*
       美しき世と   *uruwashiki yo to*
       安く和すべし   *yasuku wasu beshi*

       Rely on Aiki
       to activate
       all manifest powers:
       Pacify your enviroment
       and create a beautiful world!

(4)   合気とは   *Aiki towa*
       愛の力の   *ai no chikara no*
       元にして   *moto ni shite*
       愛は益々   *ai wa masumasu*
       栄えゆくべし   *sakae yuku beshi*

       Aiki—
       the wellspring
       of love's power:
       Make the glory of that love
       ever increase!

(5)　合気とは　　　　　*Aiki towa*
　　　万和合の　　　　*yorozu wagō no*
　　　力なり　　　　　*chikara nari*
　　　たゆまず磨け　　*tayumazu migake*
　　　道の人々　　　　*michi no hitobito*

　　　　　Aiki—
　　　　　the power which
　　　　　harmonizes all things:
　　　　　Never stop polishing [that jewel],
　　　　　You who tread this Path!

(6)　惟神　　　　　　　*Kannagara*
　　　身魂は合気　　　*mitama wa aiki*
　　　即つるぎ　　　　*soku tsurugi*
　　　研げ光れよ　　　*migake hikareyo*
　　　現世の内　　　　*utsushiyo no uchi*

　　　　　The Divine Will
　　　　　permeating body and soul
　　　　　is the blade of Aiki:
　　　　　Polish it, make it shine
　　　　　throughout this world of ours!

(7)　合気とは　　　　　*Aiki towa*
　　　筆や口には　　　*fude ya kuchi niwa*
　　　つくされず　　　*tsukusarezu*
　　　言ぶれせずに　　*kotobure sezuni*
　　　悟り行え　　　　*satori okonae*

　　　　　Aiki—[its mysteries]
　　　　　can never be encompassed
　　　　　by the brush or by the mouth.
　　　　　Do not rely on words to grasp it,
　　　　　attain enlightenment through practice!

(8)   真の武は   *Shin no bu wa*
      筆や口には   *fude ya kuchi niwa*
      すべからず   *subekarazu*
      ことぶれなせば   *kotobure naseba*
      神は許さず   *kami wa yurusazu*

      True *Bu*[*dō*]
      cannot be described by
      the brush or by the mouth—
      The gods will not allow you
      to rely upon words!

(9)   武とはいえ   *Bu to wa ie*
      声もすがたも   *koe mo sugata mo*
      影もなし   *kage mo nashi*
      神に聞かれて   *kami ni kikarete*
      答うすべなし   *kotau subenashi*

      Bu[*dō*]—
      no voice, no form,
      no shadow:
      Question the gods as you like
      but they will not reply.

(10) 声もなく   *Koe mo naku*
      心も見えず   *kokoro mo miezu*
      惟神   *kannagara*
      神に問われて   *kami ni towarete*
      何物もなし   *nanimono mo nashi*

      No voice,
      no heart to see:
      Just follow the Divine
      and there will be nothing
      to ask of the gods.

(11) 声も見ず   *Koe mo mizu*
　　　心も聞かじ   *kokoro mo kikaji*
　　　剣業   *tsurugiwaza*
　　　世を初めたる   *yo o hajimetaru*
　　　神に習ひて   *kami ni naraite*

> No voice to see,
> no heart to hear:
> The true techniques.
> Initially the world
> learned directly from the gods.*

Dōka nine, ten, and eleven are much like Zen *kōan*. Number eleven especially turns rational reasoning on its head, challenging us to return directly to the Source, and to experience the techniques first-hand just like the heroes of old who were in closer contact with the gods. *Tsurugi* literally means "sword" but since the word connotes all the different physical elements of Aikidō, I have translated it here (and in subsequent poems where the word appears) as "true techniques." That phrase may be understood as being synonymous with Aikidō.

(12) 武産は   *Takemusu wa*
　　　御親の火水に   *mioya no iki ni*
　　　合気して   *aiki shite*
　　　その営みは   *sono itonami wa*
　　　岐美の神業   *Gimi no kamuwaza*

> *Takemusu* is the
> harmonization of
> Creation's fire and water;
> that interaction is the
> Divine Techniques of GI and MI.*

*As explained in Chapter One, *Takemusu* is the procreative power of Aikidō; the phrase translated as "Creation" literally means "Exalted Parents"; and GI and MI stand for *Izanagi* and *Izanami*, the primordial male and female principles. The interaction of fire and water, male and female, left and right, gives birth to the Divine Techniques of Aikidō.

(13) 気の御わざ   *Ki no miwaza*
      赤白魂や   *akashiro tama ya*
      ますみ玉   *masumi tama*
      合気の道は   *aiki no michi wa*
      小戸の神技   *odo no kamuwaza*

> The exalted techniques of *ki*:
> Red, white,
> and crystal-clear jewels—
> they reveal the Path of Aiki,
> and the Divine Techniques of ODO.*

*This was one of Morihei's favorite *dōka*, a poem replete with complex symbolism. The red and white jewels refer to a tale in the *Kojiki* (1:44). The Sea-Deity presented another god with the red *shio-mitsu-tama* ("tide-flowing jewel") and the white *shio-hiru-tama* ("tide-ebbing jewel"). These magic jewels could cause the tide to ebb or flow at one's command, enabling the possessor to threaten an enemy with drowning, but also to save any foe who relented.

To Morihei, the red and white jewels are key to the Path of Aiki. To hold the red and white jewels is to comprehend and become one with the ebb and flow of the tides, to master the Breath of Heaven and Earth, and to flow with cosmic energy. The red and white also represent the sexual integration which gives birth to all things: the red ovum united with the white seed. Similarly, blood—the life essence—is the inner tide of red and white blood cells. When the red jewel and the white jewel are thus joined on all levels, an invincible diamond body is created, and the crystal-clear jewel of nonattachment and enlightenment emerges.

ODO is the middle of the river where *Izanagi* went to purify himself (*misogi*) after his dreadful visit to the ugly and foul world of the dead (*Kojiki* 1:11). Morihei equated ODO with 音 *oto*, the all-powerful sound of the *kototama*. Furthermore, ODO is not any particular place but exists wherever true *misogi* is performed. When *kototama* and *misogi* are conducted in unison (= ODO), the divine techniques of Aikidō appear. Morihei also explained ODO as being comprised of the *kototama* O, "emptiness," and DO, "deep concentration." Hence, ODO is a state in which one is "settled in emptiness" and thus capable of eliminating all contention and fighting. Another connotation of ODO is the "narrow gate to truth"— one must make a great effort to get through it. Regarding the

Divine Techniques of ODO Morihei stated, "When I stand in the *dōjō* I let the power of *kototama* and the energy of *Takemusu* circulate within and all about me—this generates the Divine Techniques of ODO right where I am."

(14) 現し世と   *Utsushiyo to*
　　　神や仏の   *kami ya hotoke no*
　　　道守る   *michi mamoru*
　　　合気の技は   *aiki no waza wa*
　　　草薙ののり   *kusanagi no nori*

> Protecting the Way
> of gods and buddhas
> in this world of ours:
> The techniques of Aiki
> are the law of *kusanagi*.*

Kusanagi is a reference to the *kusanagi-no-tsurugi*, "Grass-quelling Sword." This miraculous sword was discovered by *Susano-o* in the tail of the eight-headed dragon he killed (*Kojiki* 1:19). Also known as *Ame-no-murakumo-no-tsurugi*, the sword was later presented to Prince Yamato-take who used it to quell a moor-fire that threatened him by cutting down the tall grass in the field (*Kojiki* 2:83). It is reckoned as one of the Three Imperial Regalia, along with the Eight-Sided Mirror and the Curved Jewel. In Morihei's system, *kusanagi-no-tsurugi* stands for the two-sided sword of deep learning and bravery that must be wielded to protect the earth and all its inhabitants.

(15) 神習う   *Kami narau*
　　　道のしくみは   *michi no shikumi wa*
　　　惟神   *kannagara*
　　　合気の道や   *aiki no michi ya*
　　　伊都能売の神   *Izunome no kami*

> Taught to us by the gods,
> the grand design of the Path
> follows the Divine:
> The Path of Aiki [is the work of the]
> Angel of Purification!*

*The "Angel of Purification" is *Izunome-no-kami*, a deity formed to purify *Izanagi* of filth (*Kojiki* 1:11). *Izunome* is related to the wedded gods *Haya-akitsu-hiko* (male) and *Haya-akitsu-hime* (female) who together "wash away all impurity like a mighty flowing river and swallow up all sin like a great ocean." Morihei felt *Izunome*—who is generally considered female—to be present within his own body, and Aikidō to be the manifestation of that deity's power of purification and restoration. Morihei hoped that Aikidō students would eventually realize that each and every one of them also had *Izunome* within.

(16)   ありがたや   *Arigata ya*
       伊都とみずとの   *izu to mizu tono*
       合気十   *aiki dō*
       おおしく進め   *ooshiku susume*
       瑞の御声に   *mizu no mikoe ni*

A great blessing for us:
IZU and MIZU
forming the Cross of Aiki.
Press on firmly,
guided by MIZU's Exalted Voice!*

IZU is the masculine, stern aspect of creation that gives form to the universe; MIZU is the feminine, gentle aspect that gives it function. IZU, associated with *Izanagi*, is the Father; MIZU, associated with *Izanami*, is the Mother. IZU sanctions and corrects; MIZU offers love and goodness. The two aspects intersect to shape the Cross of Aiki, which sustains the world. Morihei stated that this cross of IZU-MIZU was the basis of Aikidō.

(17)   合気とは   *Aiki towa*
       神の御姿   *kami no misugata*
       御心ぞ   *mikokoro zo*
       いずとみずとの   *izu to mizu tono*
       御親とうとし   *mioya tōtoshi*

Aiki—
the Exalted Divine Form,
the Exalted Heart!
IZU and MIZU are the
Exalted Parents.

(18)   伊都の男の
　　　　こり霊はらう
　　　　伊都魂
　　　　いかりの中に
　　　　たける雄武び

                   Izu no o no
                   koritama harau
                   izunotama
                   ikari no naka ni
                   takeru otakebi

The manly IZU
cleanses the soul;
the spirit of IZU,
bristling with ferocity,
roars bravely!*

*This is a rare example of an aggressively masculine *dōka* in which only IZU is mentioned. *Otakebi*, "roar bravely," is the name of an ancient Shintō practice in which one shouts out the name of a deity in order to "summon" its presence.

(19)   又しても
　　　　行き詰まるたび
　　　　思うかな
　　　　厳と瑞との
　　　　有難き道

                   Mata shitemo
                   ikizumaru tabi
                   omou kana
                   izu to mizu tono
                   arigataki michi

Whenever I come again
to a dead end [in training],
I bring to mind
the blessed Path of
IZU and MIZU

(20)   火と水の
　　　　合気にくみし
　　　　橋の上
　　　　大海原に
　　　　いける山彦

                   Hi to mizu no
                   aiki ni kumishi
                   hashi no ue
                   ōunabara ni
                   ikeru yamabiko

Fire and water
blended together in Aiki;
[I] stand on the Bridge
above the vast sea
as the mountain echo resounds.*

*"Bridge" is "Heaven's Floating Bridge" that links heaven and earth. Ōunabara "vast sea," is a homonym for "womb," a symbol of the plane and plain of physical existence. "Mountain echo" is *yamabiko*, the *kototama* that resound within and all around us. The response of the mountain echo is immediate, fresh, and expansive; it freely embraces any sound, in any language, in whatever manner it is delivered. Mountain echo therefore represents the ideal state of Aikidō—able to respond to, embrace, and blend with anything offered, without any conditions or preconceived notions.

(21)　おのころに　　　　*Onokoro ni*
　　　常立なして　　　　*tokotachi nashite*
　　　中に生く　　　　　*naka ni iku*
　　　愛の構えは　　　　*ai no kamae wa*
　　　山彦の道　　　　　*yamabiko no michi*

> On this very earth
> stand as firmly as a god.
> Flourish in the very center—
> the stance of love is the
> Path of the mountain echo!*

Onokoro (usually pronounced "*onogoro*") means "self-congealed." It was the first island of Japan to be created, and symbolizes this present world of ours—the realm in which we must exercise individual freedom. "Stand as firmly as a god" refers to the appearance of the deity *Tokotachi-no-kami* on *Onokoro*, an outpouring of growth and vitality, and an act that is eternally recreated in Aikidō training.

(22)　天地に　　　　　　*Ametsuchi ni*
　　　気結びなして　　　*kimusubi nashite*
　　　中に立ち　　　　　*naka ni tachi*
　　　心構えは　　　　　*kokoro gamae wa*
　　　山彦の道　　　　　*yamabiko no michi*

> Link yourself to
> heaven and earth;
> stand in the very center
> with your heart receptive
> to the resounding mountain echo.

(23)   日地月　　　　　　*Hi tsuchi tsuki*
　　　　合気になりし　　　*aiki ni narishi*
　　　　橋の上　　　　　　*hashi no ue*
　　　　大海原は　　　　　*ōunabara wa*
　　　　山彦の道　　　　　*yamabiko no michi*

　　　　　　Sun, earth, and moon
　　　　　　harmonized perfectly;
　　　　　　on the bridge
　　　　　　above the vast sea
　　　　　　the mountain echo Path [leads me].

(24)   天地人　　　　　　*Tenchijin*
　　　　和合の守り　　　　*wagō no mamori*
　　　　合気道　　　　　　*aikidō*
　　　　大海原は　　　　　*ōunabara wa*
　　　　祝ぎの音　　　　　*kotohogi no oto*

　　　　　　Heaven, earth, and humankind
　　　　　　brought together and
　　　　　　protected by Aikidō—
　　　　　　throughout the vast sea [of existence]
　　　　　　a sound of great joy.

(25)   天と地と　　　　　*Ten to chi to*
　　　　神と人とを　　　　*kami to hito to o*
　　　　むつまじく　　　　*mutsumajiku*
　　　　結び合わせて　　　*musubi awasete*
　　　　み代を守らん　　　*miyo o mamoran*

　　　　　　Keep heaven, earth,
　　　　　　god, and humankind
　　　　　　in perfect harmony,
　　　　　　blended and bound together
　　　　　　for all eternity.

(26)   いきいのち   *Iki inochi*
        廻り栄ゆる   *mawari sakayuru*
        世の仕組   *yo no shikumi*
        たまの合気は   *tama no aiki wa*
        天の浮橋   *ame no ukihashi*

> Vibrant life
> circulates and vivifies
> all creation:
> The jewel-spirit of Aiki,
> Heaven's Floating Bridge.

(27)   むらきもの   *Murakimo no*
        我鍛えんと   *waga kitaen to*
        浮橋に   *ukihashi ni*
        むすぶ真空   *musubu shinkū*
        神のめぐみに   *kami no megumi ni*

> I forge myself to the
> depths of my being on
> Heaven's Floating Bridge,
> linked to True Emptiness,
> and blessed by the gods.

(28)   真空と   *Shinkū to*
        空のむすびの   *kū no musubi no*
        なかりせば   *nakariseba*
        合気の道は   *aiki no michi wa*
        知るよしもなし   *shiru yoshi mo nashi*

> If you do not
> link yourself to
> True Emptiness,
> you will never fully comprehend
> the Path of Aiki.

(29) 千早ぶる
　　　神の仕組の
　　　合（愛）気十
　　　八大力の
　　　神のさむはら

Chihayaburu
kami no shikumi no
ai (ai) ki jū
hachidairiki no
kami no samuhara

> Brave and intrepid,
> the cross of harmony (love),
> is an instrument of the gods.
> Utilize the Eight Great Powers to sustain
> the Divine Plan [of regeneration].*

*This *dōka* has two versions, one with the character for "harmony" and one with the character for "love."

The Eight Great Powers are "movement–calm; release–solidification; retraction–extension; unification–division." The "Divine Plan of regeneration," *kami no samuhara*, is a synonym for the implementing of Aikidō.

(30) くわしほこ
　　　ちたるの国の
　　　生魂や
　　　うけひに結ぶ
　　　神のさむはら

Kuwashihoko
chitaru no kuni no
ikutama ya
ukehi ni musubu
kami no samuhara

> In the land of
> finest weapons
> living souls are tied
> to their spiritual essence,
> and accomplish the Divine Plan.*

*The finest weapons of a land are enlightened warriors who have linked themselves to heaven and earth and thus understand the true purpose of the Divine Plan.

(31) 天地の   *Ametsuchi no*
　　　精魂凝りて   *seikon korite*
　　　十字道   *jūjidō*
　　　世界和楽の   *sekai waraku no*
　　　むすぶ浮橋   *musubu ukihashi*

　　　The spiritual essence
　　　of heaven and earth
　　　congeals as the cross of our Path.
　　　The peace and happiness of the world
　　　is linked to Heaven's Floating Bridge.

(32) 主の御親   *Su no mioya*
　　　至愛の心   *shiai no kokoro*
　　　大みそら   *ōmisora*
　　　世の営みの   *yo no itonami no*
　　　元となりぬる   *moto to narinuru*

　　　SU, Exalted Parent,
　　　with a heart of love
　　　as vast as the sky—
　　　it is the source of all that
　　　functions in this world.*

*This and the following series of *dōka* describe the potent power of *kototama*.

(33) 美しき   *Uruwashiki*
　　　この天地の   *kono ametsuchi no*
　　　御姿は   *misugata wa*
　　　主のつくりし   *nushi no tsukurishi*
　　　一家なりけり   *ikka narikeri*

　　　How beautiful,
　　　this form of
　　　heaven and earth—
　　　all created by the Lord,
　　　we are members of one family.*

*The character for "Lord" can also be read SU, so the third line could be translated as "all emanating from the same Source."

(34)　一霊の　　　　　*Ichirei no*
　　　元の御親の　　*moto no mioya no*
　　　御姿は　　　　*misugata wa*
　　　響き光りてぞ　*hibiki hikarite zo*
　　　生りし言霊　　*narishi kototama*

> The One Spirit,
> forming our
> original Parents—
> *kototama*, resounding everywhere,
> so fertile and bright!

(35)　大御神　　　　*Ōikami*
　　　七十五声を　　*nanasoitsukoe o*
　　　生みなして　　*umi nashite*
　　　世の経綸を　　*yo no keirin o*
　　　さずけ給えり　*sazuke tamaeri*

> From the Divine Source
> seventy-five sounds
> were born,
> activating the world
> and imparting all truth.

(36)　緒結びの　　　*Omusubi no*
　　　七十五つの　　*nanasoitsutsu no*
　　　御姿は　　　　*misugata wa*
　　　合気となりて　*aiki to narite*
　　　世をば清めつ　*yo oba kiyometsu*

> The seventy-five strings
> that hold this
> sacred creation together
> are manifest as Aiki,
> a vehicle to purify the world.

(37)   あかき血の   *Akaki chi no*
        たぎる言霊   *tagiru kototama*
        姿こそ   *sugata koso*
        妙なる道は   *taenaru michi wa*
        さむはらのほこ   *samuhara no hoko*

        The very form of
        kototama seething
        with red blood is the
        wondrous Path, and the
        true weapons of the Divine Plan.*

*Morihei often spoke of his *kototama* practice as activating the red blood within his body, how it seethed with energy and gave birth to the techniques of Aiki—the best weapons with which to arm oneself.

(38)   ことたまの   *Kototama no*
        宇内にたぎる   *udai ni tagiru*
        さむはらの   *samuhara no*
        大海原は   *ōunabara wa*
        山彦の道   *yamabiko no michi*

        Kototama—
        seething throughout the cosmos:
        In the plains of Heaven,
        in the deep sea,
        one vast mountain echo!

(39)   根元の   *Kongen no*
        気はみちみちて   *ki wa michimichite*
        乾坤や   *kenkon ya*
        造化もここに   *zōka mo koko ni*
        はじめけるかな   *hajime kerukana*

        At the Source,
        ki, rich and abundant;
        the creation of
        the universe
        began right there.

(40) 気の御わざ   *Ki no miwaza*
　　　魂の鎮めや   *tama no shizume ya*
　　　みそぎ技   *misogi waza*
　　　導き給え   *michibiki tamae*
　　　天地の神   *ametsuchi no kami*

The exalted techniques of *ki*
calm the soul, and are
vehicles of purification—
guide us to them,
O gods of heaven and earth!

(41) 気の御わざ   *Ki no miwaza*
　　　おろちの霊出や   *orochi no hide ya*
　　　蜂の霊出   *hachi no hide*
　　　たまの霊出ふる   *tama no hide furu*
　　　武産の道   *Takemusu no michi*

The exalted techniques of *ki*
can calm snakes
and charm bees.
Controlling the spirit is the
Path of *Takemusu.**

*This refers to a rite of exorcism in the *Kojiki* (1:23). One who is brave,
wise, and compassionate can tame savage beasts with techniques of Aiki.

(42) ふとまにと   *Futomani to*
　　　神習いゆく   *kami narai yuku*
　　　みそぎ業   *misogi waza*
　　　神の立てたる   *kami no tatetaru*
　　　合気なりけり   *aiki narikeri*

Techniques of purification
taught by *futomani*
and the gods.
Aiki[dō] was established
by the Divine.

(43)   まよいなば   *Mayoi naba*
       悪しき道にも   *ashiki michi nimo*
       入りぬべし   *irinu beshi*
       心の駒に   *kokoro no koma ni*
       手綱ゆるすな   *tazuna yurusuna*

       Lose your way
       and you will
       enter a bad path;
       do not give rein to the
       wild stallion of your heart.

(44)   魂のあか   *Tama no aka*
       破れ衣を   *yabure goromo o*
       とりのぞき   *torinozoki*
       天の運化に   *ame no unka ni*
       開き光れよ   *hiraki hikare yo*

       Cast off the
       tattered robes that
       stain your soul!
       Open yourself to Heaven's dictates
       and shine brightly!

(45)   天かけり   *Amakakeri*
       光の神は   *hikari no kami wa*
       降りたちぬ   *oritachinu*
       かがやきわたる   *kagayaki wataru*
       海の底にも   *umi no soko nimo*

       The Divine Light
       that spans Heaven
       must descend to earth,
       and illuminate everything
       right to the bottom of the sea.

(46) 三千年の   *Michitose no*
      御親の仕組   *mioya no shikumi*
      成り終えぬ   *nari oenu*
      よさしのままに   *yosashi no mamani*
      吾はしとめん   *ware wa shitomen*

Built up over eons,
this endless
Divine Creation.
I vow never to mar
its goodness.

(47) 道人の   *Dōjin no*
      するどく光る   *surudoku hikaru*
      御剣（御心）は   *mitsurugi (mikokoro) wa*
      身魂の中に   *mitama no naka ni*
      ひそむ悪魔に   *hisomu akuma ni*

The penetrating brilliance
of true techniques applied by
those of the Path
strikes at the evil one lurking
within their own bodies and minds.*

*As mentioned earlier, *tsurugi* is translated as "true techniques" rather than simply "sword." Another version of this *dōka* has "The penetrating brilliance / of the Exalted Mind displayed by / those of the Path. . ."

(48) すみきりし   *Sumikirishi*
      鋭く光る   *surudoku hikaru*
      御心は   *mikokoro wa*
      悪魔の巣くう   *akuma no suku u*
      すきとてもなし   *suki totemo nashi*

Crystal clear,
sharp and bright,
the Exalted Heart
allows no opening
for evil to roost.

(49) 朝日さす   *Asahi sasu*
      心もさえて   *kokoro mo saete*
      窓により   *mado ni yori*
      天かけりゆく   *amakakeri yuku*
      天照るの吾れ   *amateru no ware*

      The morning sun
      floods my heart with light.
      From my window
      I soar to Heaven
      bathed in Divine radiance.

(50) 日々に   *Nichinichi ni*
      鍛えて磨き   *kitaete migaki*
      またにごり   *mata nigori*
      雄叫びせんと   *otakebi sento*
      八大力王   *hachidairiki ō*

      Day after day,
      forge and polish yourself.
      When things get muddled
      give a mighty shout and summon
      the King of Eight Powers [within]!

(51) 山水に   *Sansui ni*
      あたりて立たぬ   *atarite tatanu*
      岩声こそ   *ganshō koso*
      清くことふる   *kiyoku kotofuru*
      人もなければ   *hito mo nakereba*

      Stand in the heart
      of nature—
      the sound of water splashing
      against the rocks is so purifying
      even if no one is there. . .

(52)　世の初め　　　　　*Yo no hajime*
　　　降し給いし　　　*kudashi tamaishi*
　　　璽鏡剣　　　　　*jikyōken*
　　　国を建ます　　　*kuni o tatemasu*
　　　神の御心　　　　*kami no mikokoro*

> At the beginning of the world
> Mirror, Jewel, and Sword
> descended, thereby
> establishing the nation
> as an expression of the Divine Mind.*

*The Mirror, Jewel, and Sword comprise the Three Regalia of the Japanese imperial line. Morihei explained the real significance of the regalia as follows: "The Mirror symbolizes knowledge and honesty; the Jewel stands for benevolence and compassion; the Sword represents bravery and resolution."

(53)　三千世界　　　　　*Sanzen sekai*
　　　一度に開く　　　*ichido ni hiraku*
　　　梅の花　　　　　*ume no hana*
　　　二度の岩戸は　　*nido no iwato wa*
　　　開かれにけり　　*hirakare nikeri*

> Amid three thousand worlds
> a single plum flower
> blooms—
> the stone door will
> open a second time.*

*Although the ideas expressed in this *dōka* are derived from Shintō mythology (*Kojiki* 17) and Ōmoto-kyō beliefs, in Morihei's idiom it means: "Aikidō, a rare flower now in bloom throughout the universe, gives us the means to open the stone door of darkness and ignorance; through the combined efforts of good people everywhere the polluted world of death and destruction will be bathed once more in the sunbeams of truth and beauty." The plum blossom is a symbol of resurrection and renewal, and it blooms whenever Aikidō is truly practiced.

(54) 招きよせ   *Maneki yose*
      風をおこして   *kaze o okoshite*
      なぎはらい   *nagi harai*
      練り直しゆく   *neri naoshi yuku*
      神の愛気に   *kami no aiki ni*

      Stir up a
      strong wind with
      the *nagi* sword and
      set things aright in
      accordance with Divine Love.*

*The "*nagi* sword" refers to the *kusanagi-no-tsurugi* (see 14).

(55) 時は今   *Toki wa ima*
      天火水地や   *ten ka sui chi ya*
      玉の緒の   *tama no o no*
      筋を正して   *suji o tadashite*
      立つぞ案内に   *tatsu zo anai ni*

      Now is the time!
      Strengthen and restore
      the cords that bind
      heaven, fire, water, and earth.
      Come stand together with me!

(56) 世の中を   *Yo no naka o*
      眺めては泣き   *nagamete wa naki*
      ふがいなさ   *fugai nasa*
      神の怒りに   *kami no ikari ni*
      我は勇みつ   *ware wa isamitsu*

      Looking at the
      world's sorry state
      do not whimper helplessly!
      With the wrath of the gods
      let us bravely head on!

(57) 生死とは   *Seishi towa*
      目の前なるぞ   *me no mae naru zo*
      心得て   *kokoro ete*
      吾ひくとても   *ware hiku totemo*
      敵は許さじ   *teki wa yurusaji*

      Keep in mind that
      life and death are
      right before your eyes:
      You may want to retreat
      but the enemy will not allow it.

(58) 道のため   *Michi no tame*
      まがれる敵を   *magareru teki o*
      よびさまし   *yobisamashi*
      言むけすすめ   *kotomuke susume*
      愛の剣に   *ai no tsurugi ni*

      For the sake of the Way
      bring your warped foes
      to their senses by utilizing
      words of encouragement and instruction,
      grounded in the techniques of love.*

*Literally, the last line has "sword of love." However, "sword" is taken to refer to the entire range of applied techniques.

(59) 武魂を   *Taketama o*
      養い磨け   *yashinai migake*
      世の中に   *yo no naka ni*
      道を照せよ   *michi o terase yo*
      神のまにまに   *kami no manimani*

      Foster and polish
      the warrior spirit
      while serving in the world;
      illuminate the Path in accordance
      with the Divine Will.

(60) 大宇宙　　　　　*Dai uchū*
剣の中に　　　　*tsurugi no naka ni*
武夫の　　　　　*mononofu no*
光となりて　　　*hikari to narite*
世にぞ開かん　　*yo nizo hirakan*

Warriors!
Rally round the
universal true techniques,
shine brightly and
reveal [Aikidō] to the world!

(61) いきをうけ　　　*Iki o uke*
いきをばたてる　*iki oba tateru*
もののふは　　　*mononofu wa*
愛をいのちと　　*ai o inochi to*
神のさむはら　　*kami no samuhara*

A warrior receives
the gift of life
and establishes life everywhere:
Love is life, the essence
of the Divine Plan.

(62) 神ながら　　　　*Kannagara*
天地のいきに　　*tenchi no iki ni*
まかせつつ　　　*makase tsutsu*
神へのこころを　*kami e no kokoro o*
つくせますらを　*tsukuse masurao*

Entrust yourself to the
sacred life force of
heaven and earth;
draw your heart close to the gods,
O brave warriors!

(63)　古より　　　　　　　*Furuki yori*
　　　文武の道は　　　　*bunbu no michi wa*
　　　両輪と　　　　　　*ryōrin to*
　　　稽古の徳に　　　　*keiko no toku ni*
　　　身魂悟りぬ　　　　*mitama satorinu*

　　　　　From ancient times
　　　　　deep learning and *Bu[dō]*
　　　　　have been two wheels of the Path;
　　　　　through the virtue of practice
　　　　　enlighten body and mind.

(64)　ゆるぎなく　　　　*Yurugi naku*
　　　大宇に生えし　　　*daiu ni haeshi*
　　　御剣は　　　　　　*mitsurugi wa*
　　　文武両刃と　　　　*bunbu ryōba to*
　　　かみのしくみぞ　　*kami no shikumi zo*

　　　　　Steadfast and sure,
　　　　　animating the cosmos—
　　　　　the Sword of [Aiki].
　　　　　Deep learning and *Bu[dō]*, the double-edged
　　　　　instrument of the gods' grand design.*

*In this *dōka*, *tsurugi* is translated as "sword" rather than "true techniques" due to the context.

(65)　文は又　　　　　　*Bun wa mata*
　　　表に起てる　　　　*omote ni tateru*
　　　其時は　　　　　　*sono toki wa*
　　　身魂は剣　　　　　*mitama wa tsurugi*
　　　万ず導く　　　　　*yorozu michibiku*

　　　　　When learning
　　　　　becomes superficial,
　　　　　follow the all-embracing
　　　　　guidance of the true techniques
　　　　　in body and soul.

(66) 武夫の   *Mononofu no*
      敵に向いし   *teki ni mukaishi*
      其時は   *sono toki wa*
      万法すべて   *banpō subete*
      文となりとぐ   *bun to naritogu*

When a warrior
confronts a foe,
all things serve
to make the teaching
more focused.

(67) 奇びなる   *Kushibi naru*
      剣の道の   *tsurugi no michi no*
      御経綸   *onshikumi*
      熱も光も   *netsu mo hikari mo*
      おのが心に   *onoga kokoro ni*

Mysterious is
the grand design of the
true techniques—
place its heat and light
right inside your heart.*

*As mentioned in Chapter One, Morihei often spoke of the light and heat generated by the practice of Aikidō. "Light" symbolizes "insight and clear vision"; "heat" represents "compassion and friendship."

(68) 正勝吾勝   *Masakatsu agatsu*
      御親心に   *mioyagokoro ni*
      合気して   *aiki shite*
      すくい活かすは *sukui ikasu wa*
      おのが身魂ぞ   *onoga mitama zo*

True Victory is Self Victory!
Harmonize yourself with the
Divine Parent Mind—
salvation lives right within
your own body and soul!*

*Dōka 68 through 72 have slightly irregular syllable patterns.

(69) 世を思い　　　　　*Yo o omoi*
　　　嘆きいさいつ　　*nageki isaitsu*
　　　また奮い　　　　*mata furui*
　　　むら雲の光は　　*murakumo no hikari wa*
　　　我に勝速日して　*ware ni katsuhayabi shite*

　　　　　Thinking of this world,
　　　　　I sigh with lament,
　　　　　but then I fight on,
　　　　　guided by billowing clouds of light,
　　　　　and accomplish my Day of Swift Victory!

(70) 技は　　　　　　　　*Waza wa*
　　　熱心になれば　　　*nesshin ni nareba*
　　　かくなるものと　　*kaku naru mono to*
　　　信じて錬磨すべし　*shinjite renmasu beshi*

　　　　　If you practice
　　　　　the techniques diligently,
　　　　　you will have trust in what develops
　　　　　and forge yourself accordingly.*

(71) 常々の　　　　　　*Tsunezune no*
　　　技の稽古に　　　*waza no keiko ni*
　　　心せよ　　　　　*kokoro seyo*
　　　一を以て　　　　*hitotsu o motte*
　　　万に当るぞ　　　*yorozu ni ataru zo*
　　　修業者の道　　　*shugyōsha no michi*

　　　　　Over and over,
　　　　　train in the techniques
　　　　　with all your heart.
　　　　　Use the One
　　　　　to strike the Many:
　　　　　This is the Path of a real practitioner.

(72) 呼びさます   *Yobi samasu*
      一人の相手も   *hitori no aite mo*
      心せよ   *kokoro seyo*
      一を以て   *hitotsu o motte*
      万に当る   *yorozu ni ataru*
      武夫の道   *masurao no michi*

    Even when called out
    by a single foe,
    remain on guard.
    Use the One
    to strike the Many:
    This is the Path of a warrior.

(73) 向上は   *Kōjō wa*
      秘事も稽古も   *hiji mo keiko mo*
      あらばこそ   *araba koso*
      極意のぞむな   *gokui nozomuna*
      前ぞ見えたり   *mae zo mietari*

    Progress comes to
    those who train in the
    inner and outer factors.
    Do not chase after "secret techniques,"
    for everything is right before your eyes!

(74) あるとあれ   *Aru to are*
      太刀習って   *tachi naratte*
      何かせん   *nanika sen*
      唯一筋に   *tada hitosuji ni*
      思い斬るべし   *omoi kiru beshi*

    Learning this or that
    sword technique—
    of what use can it be?
    Just single-mindedly
    cut right to [the heart of things].

(75) 教には 　　　　　*Oshie niwa*
　　　打ち突く拍子 　　*uchitsuku hyōshi*
　　　さとく聞け 　　　*satoku kike*
　　　極意のけいこ 　　*gokui no keiko*
　　　表なりけり 　　　*omote narikeri*

Learn to sense the
rhythm of attacking
thrusts and cuts:
The secrets of training
lie right on the surface.

(76) 己が身に 　　　　*Onoga mi ni*
　　　ひそめる敵を 　　*hisomeru teki o*
　　　エイと斬り 　　　*EI to kiri*
　　　ヤアと物皆 　　　*YAA to monomina*
　　　イエイと導け 　　*IEI to michibike*

To the enemy
lurking within—
cut with EI!
receive with YAA!
and guide with IEI!*

*Regarding *kiai*, vigorous shouts used in the traditional martial arts of Japan, Morihei said, "In classical swordsmanship, swordsmen cut with EI, received with YAA, and separated with TOH. When there was no opening on either side, the swordsmen withdrew with TOH. Such shouts were used to develop a keen sense of timing."

(77) 物見をば 　　　　*Monomi oba*
　　　ヤという声を 　　*YA to iu koe o*
　　　拍子つつ 　　　　*hyōshi tsutsu*
　　　敵の拍子に 　　　*teki no hyōshi ni*
　　　うつりかはるな 　*utsuri kawaru na*

See things clearly,
shout YA! and
pick up the beat.
Do not follow
your opponent's lead.

(78)   せん太刀を   Sentachi o
      天に構えて   ten ni kamaete
      早くつめ   hayaku tsume
      打ち逃しなば   uchi nogashi naba
      横に斬るべし   yoko ni kiru beshi

      The controlling sword
      assumes the stance of Heaven.
      Quickly move in,
      strike and evade,
      cutting to all sides!

(79)   敵の太刀   Teki no tachi
      弱くなさんと   yowaku nasan to
      思いなば   omoi naba
      まず踏み込みて   mazu fumikomite
      敵を斬るべし   teki o kiru beshi

      If you want to
      disarm your foe,
      seize the initiative
      step in
      and cut decisively!

(80)   左右をば   Sayū oba
      斬るも払うも   kiru mo harau mo
      打ちすてて   uchi sutete
      人の心は   hito no kokoro wa
      すぐに馳せ行け   sugu ni hase ike

      Left and right,
      single-mindedly
      slash through
      all cuts and parries:
      Rush in [and control the attack]!

(81) すきもなく   *Suki mo naku*
たたきつめたる   *tataki tsume taru*
敵の太刀   *teki no tachi*
みな打ちすてて   *mina uchisutete*
踏み込みて斬れ   *fumikomite kire*

Free of weakness
slash through
the sharp attacks
of your foes:
Step in and cut!

(82) 敵人の   *Tekibito no*
走り来たりて   *hashiri kitarite*
打つときは   *utsu toki wa*
一足よけて   *issoku yokete*
すぐに斬るべし *sugu ni kiru beshi*

When your opponents
run in
to attack,
take one step aside
and immediately cut.

(83) 前後とは   *Zengo towa*
穂先いしづき   *hosaki ishizuki*
敵ぞかし   *teki zo kashi*
槍を小楯に   *yari o kotate ni*
斬り込み勝つべし *kirikomi katsu beshi*

Front and back
surrounded by long spears!
Use the enemy's weapons
as your shield—
cut in and attain victory!

(84)   取りまきし   *Torimakishi*
        槍の林に   *yari no hayashi ni*
        入るときは   *iru toki wa*
        小楯は己が   *kotate wa onoga*
        心とぞ知れ   *kokoro tozo shire*

When surrounded
by a forest
of spears,
know that you must use
your own mind as a shield.

(85)   立ちむかう   *Tachimukau*
        剣の林を   *ken no hayashi o*
        導くに   *michibiku ni*
        小楯は敵の   *kotate wa teki no*
        心とぞ知れ   *kokoro tozo shire*

Confronted by a
forest of swords,
guide the attacks:
Know that you must use the
minds of your opponents as a shield.

(86)   敵多勢   *Teki tazei*
        我をかこみて   *ware o kakomite*
        攻むるとも   *semuru tomo*
        一人の敵と   *hitori no teki to*
        思いたたかえ   *omoi tatakae*

A host of enemies
encircle me and attack:
Thinking of them
as a single foe
I wage the battle.

(87) まが敵に　　　　　*Magateki ni*
　　　斬りつけさせて　*kiritsuke sasete*
　　　吾が姿　　　　　*waga sugata*
　　　後に立ちて　　　*ushiro ni tachite*
　　　敵を斬るべし　　*teki o kiru beshi*

　　　　　Letting the
　　　　　warped foe
　　　　　strike at my form,
　　　　　I slip behind him
　　　　　and counterattack.

(88) 太刀ふるい　　　*Tachi furui*
　　　前にあるかと　　*mae ni aru ka to*
　　　襲い来る　　　　*osoi kuru*
　　　敵の後に　　　　*teki no ushiro ni*
　　　吾は立ちけり　　*ware wa tachikeri*

　　　　　Seeing me before him
　　　　　the enemy raises his sword
　　　　　to strike,
　　　　　but by that time
　　　　　I already stand behind him.

(89) 鬼おろち　　　　*Oni orochi*
　　　吾に向いて　　　*ware ni mukaite*
　　　おそいこば　　　*osoi koba*
　　　後に立ちて　　　*ushiro ni tachite*
　　　愛にみちびけり　*ai ni michibikeri*

　　　　　As soon as the
　　　　　Demon Snake
　　　　　attacks
　　　　　I am already behind it
　　　　　guiding [evil] with love.

(90)　ふりまわす　　　*Furimawasu*
　　　太刀に目付けて　*tachi ni metsukete*
　　　何かせん　　　　*nanika sen*
　　　拳は人の　　　　*kobushi wa hito no*
　　　斬るところたれ　*kiru tokoro tare*

Of what use is it
to fix your gaze on
your opponent's sword?
It is his hands that reveal
where he will cut.

(91)　下段をば　　　　*Gedan oba*
　　　陽の心を　　　　*yō no kokoro o*
　　　陰に見て　　　　*in ni mite*
　　　打ち突く剣を　　*uchitsuku ken o*
　　　清眼と知れ　　　*seigan to shire*

Take the *gedan* stance,
perceive the heart of *yang*
as being in *yin*:
Know that cuts and thrusts
originate from *seigan*.*

*This and the following two *dōka* deal with the technical aspects of swordsmanship.

Gedan is a stance in which the sword is held at a lower position; *chūdan* is a middle-level stance; and in *jōdan* the sword is held high above the head. *Seigan* is the normal, natural stance assumed when one holds a sword.

(92) 中段は
　　　敵の心を
　　　その中に
　　　うつり調子を
　　　同じ拳に

　　　Chūdan wa
　　　teki no kokoro o
　　　sono naka ni
　　　utsurichōshi o
　　　onaji kobushi ni

> In *chūdan*
> shift your opponent's mind
> right to the middle:
> Time your movements
> to match his fists.

(93) 上段は
　　　敵の心を
　　　踏み定め
　　　陰の心を
　　　陽にこそ見れ

　　　Jōdan wa
　　　teki no kokoro o
　　　fumi sadame
　　　in no kokoro o
　　　yō ni koso mire

> In *jōdan*
> step in and seize control
> of your opponent's mind:
> Perceive the heart of *yin*
> as being in *yang*.

(94) 右手をば
　　　陽にあらわし
　　　左手は
　　　陰にかえして
　　　相手みちびけ

　　　Migite oba
　　　yō ni arawashi
　　　hidarite wa
　　　in ni kaeshite
　　　aite michibike

> In the right hand
> manifest *yang*;
> in the left hand
> turn to *yin*
> and lead your partner.

(95) 松竹梅　　　　　*Shōchikubai*
錬り清めゆく　　　*neri kiyome yuku*
気の仕組　　　　　*ki no shikumi*
いずこに生るや　　*izuko ni naru ya*
身変るの火水　　　*mikawaru no iki*

Pine, Bamboo, Plum—
they refine and purify, and
form the basis of *ki*.
From where do they arise?
In the transformations of fire and water.*

*The evergreen pine is associated with the Jewel, completeness, the square, and *Katsuhayabi*; the sturdy bamboo is associated with the Sword, resilience, the circle, and *Agatsu*; and the elegant plum blossom is associated with the Mirror, stability, the triangle, and *Masakatsu*.

(96) 六合の　　　　　*Rikugō no*
内限りなくぞ　　　*uchi kagirinaku zo*
かきめぐり　　　　*kaki meguri*
きよめの道は　　　*kiyome no michi wa*
〇ともちろに　　　*maru to mochiro ni*

The universe
has no boundaries,
it turns and turns:
Our Path of purity
fills the circle [of life].

(97) 誠をば
　　　更に誠に
　　　練り上げて
　　　顕幽一如の
　　　真諦を知れ

Makoto oba
sara ni makoto ni
neriagete
kenyū ichijo no
shintai o shire

> Sincerity!
> Cultivate yourself
> sincerely and thus realize
> the profound truth that
> manifest and hidden are one.

(98) 人は皆
　　　何とあるとも
　　　覚悟して
　　　粗忽に太刀を
　　　出すべからず

Hito wa mina
nan to aru tomo
kakugo shite
sokotsu ni tachi o
idasu bekarazu

> One who is
> enlightened
> to all things
> will have no need
> to draw his sword rashly.

(99) 惟神
　　　合気のわざを
　　　極むれば
　　　如何なる敵も
　　　襲うすべなし

Kannagara
aiki no waza o
kiwamureba
ikanarunaru teki mo
osou sube nashi

> Master the Divine
> Techniques of Aiki
> and no foe
> will dare
> to challenge you.

(100)   合気とは   *Aiki towa*
        解けばむつかし   *tokeba mutsukashi*
        道なれど   *michi naredo*
        ありのままなる   *arinomama naru*
        天のめぐりよ   *ame no meguri yo*

Aiki—
a Path so difficult
to comprehend,
yet as simple as
the natural flow of Heaven.

PART
III

MORIHEI'S
CALLIGRAPHIC LEGACY

I n East Asia, the calligraphy of a master teacher is always revered, for it is felt that the brushstrokes are a direct expression of the master's spirit. Long after a master such as Morihei is gone his calligraphy is thought to retain his physical presence, and his brushwork continues to inspire each new generation of Aikidō students. The content of the calligraphy is also important, since the master reveals what he deems most essential by the themes he selects.

Morihei at age eighty-five brushing a *dōka*. Beginning in his mid-seventies, Morihei composed many splendid pieces of calligraphy for disciples, friends, and admirers.

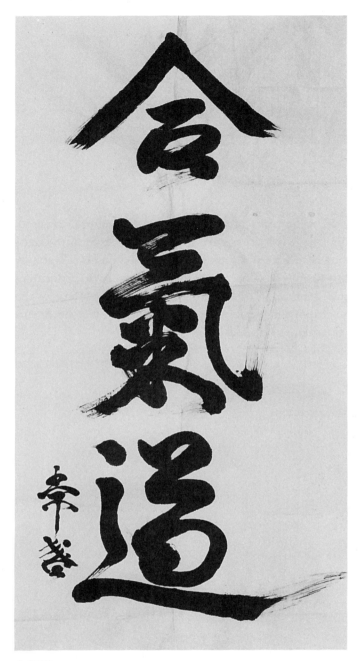

合氣道
常盛
Aikidō / Tsunemori
"Aikidō, [signed] Tsunemori."
This piece, composed in Morihei's mid-seventies, is tight and controlled.

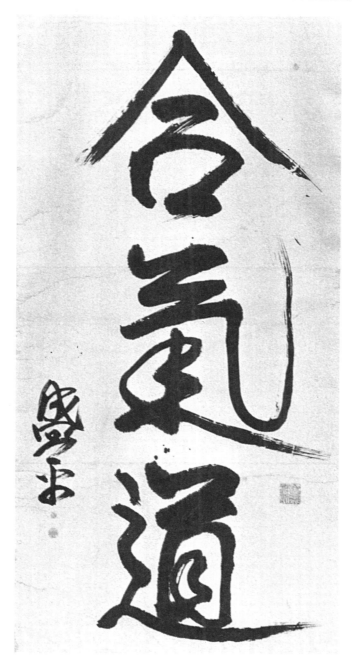

合氣道
　盛平

Aikidō / Morihei

"Aikidō, [signed] Morihei."

This scroll, which hangs in the main training hall of the Aikikai International Headquarters, was done when Morihei was in his eighties. As a master grows older, his spirit expands; evident in this work are the depth and extension of Morihei's "Way of Harmony" in his final years.

Morihei considered himself to be an incarnation of the divine principles brushed below. In these works he emphasizes that Aikidō has the power to transform anyone who trains sincerely in a similar way.

合氣道
　武産合氣翁
　常盛
Aikidō / Takemusu Aiki Ō Tsunemori

"Aikidō, [signed] Tsunemori, the old-fellow Takemusu Aiki."

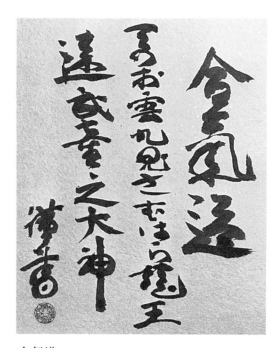

合氣道
　天の村雲九鬼さむはら龍王
　速武産之大神
　謹書
Aikidō / Ame-no-murakumo-kuki-samuhara Ryūō / Haya-takemusu-no-ōkami / Kinsho

"Aikidō: Respectfully brushed by [the incarnation of the] Great Spirit *Haya-takemusu-Ame-no-murakumo-kuki-samuhara Ryūō*."

合氣大神
　盛平謹書
Aiki Ōkami / Morihei kinsho
　"Great Spirit of Aiki, respectfully brushed by Morihei."
Aikidō is the particular Path we follow in this world; the Great
Spirit of Aiki is the universal Way that permeates the cosmos.

Moriei once said, "*Takemusu Aiki* will let you know if your techniques are alive or dead," and he frequently used the four characters of *Take-musu Aiki* for his calligraphic statements.

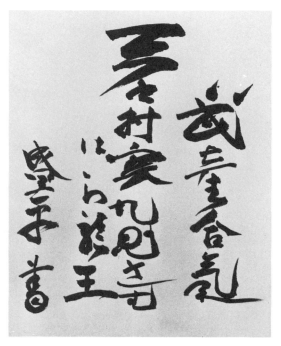

武産合氣
　天之村雲九鬼さむ
　はら龍王
　盛平書
Takemusu Aiki / Ame-no-murakumo-kuki-samu / hara Ryūō / Morihei sho
"*Takemusu Aiki*, brushed by Morihei, [incarnation of] *Ame-no-murakumo-kuki-samuhara Ryūō.*"

武産合氣
　盛平
Takemusu Aiki / Morihei
"*Takemusu Aiki*, [signed] Morihei."

勝吾勝正
　盛平
Masakatsu Agatsu / Morihei
　"True Victory is Self-Victory, [signed] Morihei."
This work features one of the many mottos that Morihei
often brushed for his disciples.

In the practice of Aikidō, there should be a natural progression from *Bujutsu* (martial techniques) to *Budō* (martial path of virtue) to *Bushin* (martial sacraments of divine transformation).

天の村雲九鬼さむはら龍王
武神
盛平謹書
Ame-no-murakumo-kuki-samuhara Ryūō / Bushin / Morihei kinsho
"*Ame-no-murakumo-kuki-samuhara Ryūō,* Divine *Bu,* respectfully brushed by Morihei."

武神
常盛謹書
Bushin / Tsunemori kinsho
"Divine *Bu,* respectfully brushed by Tsunemori."

神氣宇内涌立

　常盛翁

Shinki udai waki tatsu / Tsunemori Ō

"Divine *ki* wells up and fills the universe! [signed] the old-fellow Tsunemori."

Bristling with *ki*, this piece manifests the meaning of the calligraphy in the very brushstrokes.

氣

　常盛

Ki (musubi) / Tsunemori

"*Ki (musubi)*, [signed] Tsunemori."

This truly delightful piece has a little knot in the tail representing *musubi*, "tying-up of the life force."

生気
　常盛
Seiki / Tsunemori
　"Life Force, [signed] Tsunemori."
Seiki connotes vitality, animation, and spiritedness.

These pieces feature two versions of the *dōka* Morihei most frequently brushed; it is likely that he considered it as the best means of expressing the key to his teaching.

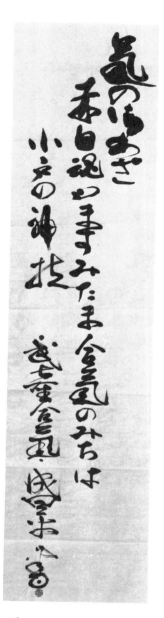

惟神武産
　赤白たまやますみ
　たま
　合氣の道は
　小戸の
　神技　盛平

Kannagara Takemusu / akashiro tama ya masumi / tama / aiki no michi wa / odo no / kamu waza Morihei

"The Divine Will [manifest as] *Takemusu*: Red, white, and crystal-clear jewels—they reveal the path of Aiki, and the Divine Techniques of ODO, [brushed by] Morihei."

氣の御わざ
　赤白魂やますみたま合氣のみちは
　小戸の神技　武産合氣盛平書

Ki no miwaza / akashiro tama ya masumi tama aiki no michi wa / odo no kamu waza Takemusu Aiki Morihei

"The exalted techniques of *ki*: Red, white, and crystal-clear jewels—they reveal the path of Aiki, and the Divine Techniques of ODO, [brushed by] Takemusu Aiki Morihei."

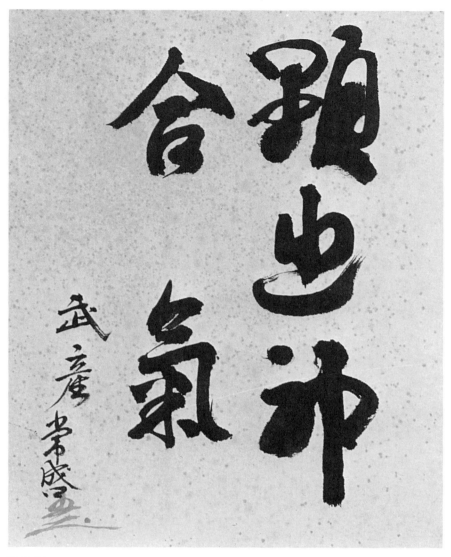

顕幽神
　合氣
　武産常盛

Ken Yū Shin / Aiki / Takemusu Tsunemori

"Manifest, Hidden, Divine: Aiki, [signed] Takemusu Tsunemori."
(The mark under Morihei's name is a *kao*, a personal cipher used in lieu of a seal.)

The manifest realm is the physical world we can see and touch; the hidden realm is the sphere of air, *ki*, and atoms; the divine realm is the holiness of creation, the innermost heart of things. The techniques of Aikidō have the same three dimensions: forms constitute the manifest realm, breath and *ki* power shape the hidden realm, and spiritual transformation creates the divine realm—then the techniques become sacraments. All three realms must be unified through Aiki.

愛光
　勝速日降下
　武産合氣
　常盛
Aikō / Katsuhayabi koka / Takemusu Aiki / Tsunemori

"Love's Light: The Day of Swift Victory has descended! [signed] Takemusu Aiki Tsunemori."

光愛天
　常盛
Ten Ai Kō / Tsunemori
"Heavenly Love and Light, [signed]
Tsunemori."

愛
Ai
"Love."

光
盛平

Hikari / Morihei

"Light, [signed] Morihei."

This is one of the last pieces of calligraphy brushed by Morihei before his death, a kind of final statement. The brushstrokes are extraordinarily lucid and clear.

PART
IV

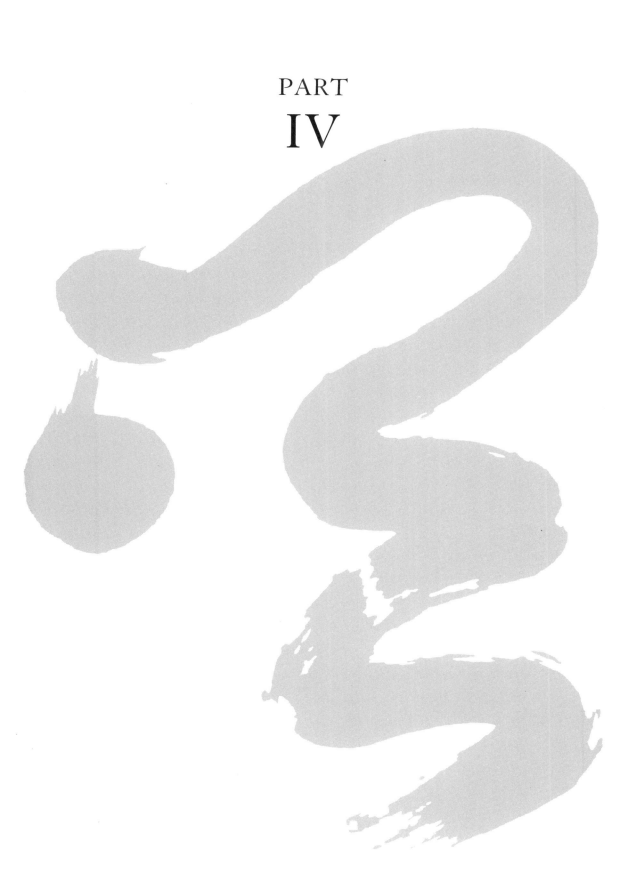

MISOGI:
Purification of Body and Mind

Morihei stated that *misogi*, "purification of body and mind," was the heart of Aikidō; in order to practice the Way of Harmony properly one must:

Calm the spirit and return to the Divine (鎮魂帰神 *chinkon-kishin*).

Cleanse the body and spirit by removing all malice, selfishness, and desire (禊 *misogi*).

Be ever-grateful for the gifts received from the universe, Mother Nature, your family, and your fellow human beings (感謝 *kansha*).

Chinkon, also pronounced *tama-shizume*, means "to settle the spirit and collect the mind." *Kishin*, "return to the Divine," is "to repose in the holiness of life."

In his later years, Morihei performed an hour-long version of *chinkon-kishin* each morning and evening (if possible outdoors) and an abbreviated version prior to training in the *dōjō*. Morihei encouraged his students to do some type of *chinkon-kishin* in order to understand Aikidō in both body and spirit. He taught:

You need *chinkon-kishin* to see the light of wisdom. Sit comfortably and first contemplate the manifest realm of existence. This realm is concerned with externals, the physical form of things.

Fill your body with *ki* and sense the manner in which the universe functions—its shape, its color, and its vibrations. Breathe in and let yourself soar to the ends of the universe; breathe out and bring the cosmos back inside. Next, breathe up all the fecundity and vibrancy of the earth. Then, blend the

Breath of Heaven and the Breath of Earth with that of your
own, becoming the Breath of Life itself. As you calm down,
naturally let yourself settle in the hidden realm of the form-
less, returning to the heart of things. Find your center, the
kototama SU, the source of the universe. Fill yourself with
light and heat. Like this, always keep your mind as bright and
clear as the vast sky, the great ocean, and the highest peak,
empty and free.

The practice of *chinkon-kishin* also involves *misogi*, the purification of
body and mind. External *misogi* is a scouring of the body with water to
wash away grime; internal *misogi* is a detoxification of the inner organs
through deep breathing; and spiritual *misogi* is a cleansing of the heart to
purge oneself of maliciousness. Morihei explained the significance of
misogi like this:

The only cure for materialism is the cleansing of the six senses
(eyes, ears, nose, tongue, body, and mind). If the senses are
clogged, one's perception is stifled. The more it is stifled, the
more contaminated the senses become. This creates disorder
in one's life and, consequently, throughout the entire world,
and that is the greatest evil of all. In order to protect the
world, we must first rid ourselves of defilements.

Morihei declared that *misogi* is needed to set things aright:

MI represents both the body and the mind, the outer and
inner aspects of a human being; SO is fleshy envelopment of
SU, the Divine spark; and GI (KI) stands for a whiteness that
is clear and unadulterated. In short, *misogi* is a washing away
of all defilements, a removal of all obstacles, a separation from
disorder, an abstention from negative thoughts, a radiant state
of unadorned purity, the accomplishment of all things, a con-
dition of lofty virtue, and a spotless environment. In *misogi*
one returns to the very beginning, where there is no differentiation between oneself and the universe.

For Morihei, the practice of Aikidō and the performance of its techniques were synonymous with *misogi*:

> Train sincerely in Aikidō and evil thoughts and deeds will naturally disappear. Daily training in Aikidō allows your inner divinity to shine brighter and brighter. Do not concern yourself with the right and wrong of others. Do not be calculating or act unnaturally. Keep your heart set on Aikidō, and do not criticize other teachers or traditions. Aikidō embraces all and purifies everything.

Chinkon-kishin and *misogi* foster *kansha*, an overwhelming sense of gratitude and reverence for life:

> Saints and sages have always revered the sacredness of heaven and earth, of mountains, rivers, trees, and grasses. They were always mindful of the great blessings of nature. They realized that it is the divine purpose of life to make the world continually afresh, to create each day anew. If you understand the principles of Aikidō you too will be glad to be alive, and you will greet each day with great joy.

Morihei performing *chinkon-kishin* prior to training. In the *dōjō* Morihei's *chinkon-kishin* was not very long, but in the morning it could last several hours and included chanting, meditation, and "salutation to the rising sun."

Morihei and his son Kisshōmaru performing *misogi* in a waterfall. One type of *misogi* is traditionally practiced beneath a waterfall, and throughout his life Morihei periodically retreated to the mountains to do such *misogi*.

Morihei conducting a formal purification rite during the opening of the Honolulu *dōjō*. On ceremonial occasions Morihei would use the *harai-gushi*, a sacred stick adorned with strips of paper, to perform *misogi*. *Misogi* creates an environment that is fresh, pure, honest, and true.

Morihei using *misogi-no-jō* to unite heaven and earth, *yin* and *yang*, and fire and water with his own body and mind. Morihei typically employed the *jō* to perform his *chinkon-kishin/misogi* before training.

Morihei displaying various postures incorporated into *misogi-no-jō*.

Morihei sometimes described *misogi-no-jō* as 天の神楽 *ame-no-kagura*, "Heaven's Divine Dance." He visualized himself standing on "Heaven's Floating Bridge," moving up and down, back and forth, with vigorous grace to expel all evil and to fill himself with peace and love.

Morihei recommended that *misogi-no-jō* should also be practiced with a partner to improve one's ability to blend with any type of attack.

Misogi executed with a sword is *misogi-no-ken*. Here, a young Morihei is showing a group of Japanese classical dance instructors how to stand with a sword. *Misogi-no-ken*, too, is a kind of beautiful Divine dance.

Morihei demonstrating *misogi-no-ken* with Kisshōmaru. Morihei called such paired techniques *Shōchikubai kenpō,* "Swordplay of Pine-Bamboo-Plum."

Morihei in his later years, moving in with a thrust of *misogi-no-ken*, piercing right to the center.

Morihei believed that "If you understand the principles of Aikidō, you will be glad to be alive, and you will greet each day with great joy."

PART

V

THE ART OF AIKIDŌ

Techniques are the vehicles used to express the spiritual principles of Aikidō. They are not set forms since "change and adaptability are the essence of Aikidō." Morihei did not say much about the technical aspects of Aikidō training, for he believed, "If your heart is true your techniques will be correct."

The most thorough technical presentation of Morihei's techniques is found in his book *Budō*. In addition to further hints contained in the *dōka*, Morihei also emphasized the following basic points to his students regarding the execution of Aikidō techniques:

Even though our Path is completely different from warrior arts of the past, it is not necessary to abandon the old ways totally. Absorb venerable traditions in Aikidō by clothing them with fresh garments, and build on the classic styles to create better forms.

Our techniques employ four qualities that reflect the nature of our world. Depending on the circumstance, you should be: hard as a diamond, flexible as a willow, smooth-flowing like water, or as empty as space.

The body should be triangular, the mind circular. The triangle represents the generation of energy and is the most stable physical posture. The circle symbolizes serenity and perfection, the source of unlimited techniques. The square stands for solidity, the basis of applied control.

A good stance and posture reflect a proper state of mind. The key to good technique is to keep your hands, feet, and hips straight and centered. If you are centered, you can move freely. The physical center is your belly; if your mind is set there as well, you are assured of victory in any endeavor.

Do not stare into the eyes of your opponent: he may mesmerize you. Do not fix your gaze on his sword: he may intimidate you. Do not focus on your opponent at all: he may absorb your energy. The essence of technique is to bring your opponent completely into your sphere. Then you can stand just where you like, in a safe and unassailable position.

When an opponent comes forward, move in and greet him; if he wants to pull back, send him on his way.

As indicated in *Budō*, the techniques of Aikidō are structured into six pillars:

> *Shihō-nage* (four-directions throws)
> *Irimi-nage* (entering throws)
> *Kaiten* (open-and-turn movements)
> *Kokyū-hō* (breath-power techniques)
> *Osae-waza* (pinning techniques)
> *Ushiro-waza* (rear techniques).

1. 四方投 *Shihō-nage*

The first of the six pillars of Aikidō techniques is *shihō-nage*. This technique represents the gratitude Aikidō trainees feel toward life in all "four directions," and it is commonly the first technique learned (but not easily mastered) by students.

1

2

3

Morihei demonstrates *shihō-nage* in a *hanmi-hantachi* form. The key to the proper execution of *shihō-nage* is to extend *ki* out through the fingertips (1), and to keep the hands, hips, and feet in a straight line (2, 3).

1

2

3

4

Two methods of neutralizing a *shōmen* or *yokomen* attack: (1) sliding at a ninety-degree angle to the outside, or (2) making a ninety-degree turn to the inside. During the throw (3) the head, hands, hips, and feet are in a straight line. The technique finishes, in this case, with a solid sitting pin (4).

1

2

The *ura* version of *shihō-nage* (1, 2). In (3) Morihei demonstrates a standing *shihō-nage* pin.

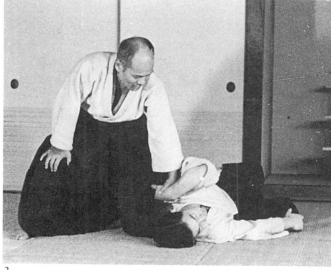

3

1

2

4

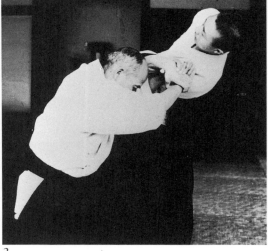

3

Another version of *hanmi-hantachi shihō-nage* (1, 2, 3, 4).

2. 入 身 投 *Irimi-nage*

Irimi, the second pillar of Aikidō techniques, means "to enter," physically and spiritually, into an attack while simultaneously sidestepping it.

1

Morihei demonstrates his dynamic *irimi* in two ways: with a sword (1) and empty-handed (2). Morihei once described the principle of *irimi* as "One Sword–One Body" (*ittō-isshin*) —entering must be straight, sharp, and true.

2

1

2

3

4

5

Morihei demonstrating perfect *irimi* with the sword (1, 2, 3). The body technique version is shown from the side (4) and from the front (5).

Atemi, a blow to neutralize an attack, is essential to good *irimi*. Here Morihei demonstrates various individual *atemi* against different types of attack in *suwari-waza*.

1

2

3

In *tachi-waza* Morihei demonstrates *atemi* against *yokomen* (1, 2) and against *shōmen* (3).

1

2

Morihei performs triangular *irimi* with a
sword (1) and as a body technique (2).

Morihei enters with a strong *atemi* (2) and finishes off with powerful triangular footwork (3) and, shown from a different angle, (4).

1

2

This bone-crunching *irimi* (1, 2) is an example of old-style
bujutsu forms which were largely modified in Aikidō.

1

2

Triangular *irimi* smoothly applied against an attempted shoulder hold (1, 2, 3, 4, 5).

3

4

5

1

2

Morihei first draws his partner out and then
pins him to the side in a variation of seated
irimi techniques (1, 2, 3).

3

1

2

In another variation of seated *irimi* techniques, Morihei first draws his partner out and then throws him over to the front (1, 2, 3).

3

1

2

Triangular *irimi* variation ending
with a pin (1, 2, 3).

3

1

2

A triangular *irimi* with throw (1, 2, 3).

3

1

2

Triangular *irimi* (1, 2) can be applied against almost any attack.

1

2

In *chokusen irimi*, "direct entering," one slides in completely behind the attack (1, 2).

1

2

Later in life, Morihei's *irimi* became more circular. He
would enter to the side (1), guide his partner around (2),
and then bring him down with a soft spiral touch (3).

3

1

2

Throughout his career, from his earliest days (1) to his final years (2), *soku-men irimi* "side approach" was one of Morihei's favorite techniques.

1

2

Seated *sokumen-irimi* (1, 2) with pin (3).

3

1

2

Variations of *sokumen-irimi* against a shoulder hold: a throw (1, 2) and a pin (3, 4).

3

4

Sokumen irimi against a spear attack. The principle is
the same against a *jō* or a sword.

3. 開 転 *Kaiten*

Kaiten, the third pillar of Aikidō, means "open and turn." In *Budō* Morihei also described these movements as *kaika*, "turn and transform," an instantaneous adjustment to any attack. In *kaiten* one must open the heart and turn around aggression.

Morihei demonstrates the concluding *kaiten* posture from two different angles (1, 2). After turning around the attack Morihei ends up facing the same direction as his partner, completely diffusing the aggression.

1

2

A *kaiten* movement to the front in a *hanmi-hantachi* technique.

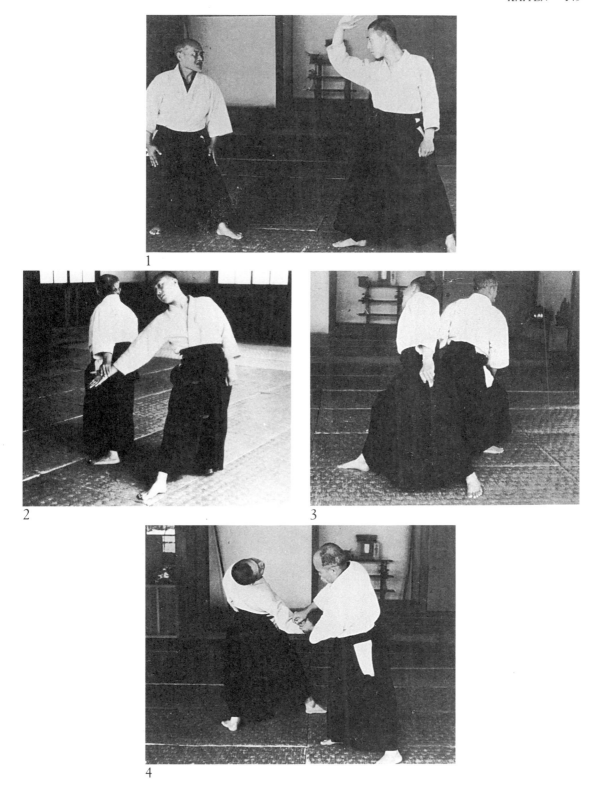

The most common application of *kaiten* is in *kote-gaeshi*. The big *kaiten* turn against a *shōmen* attack (1) is shown from two different angles (2, 3).

1

2

3

4

5

Seated *kote-gaeshi* technique (1, 2, 3, 4) with pin variation (5).

1

Kote-gaeshi variation against a sleeve
hold (1, 2, 3).

2

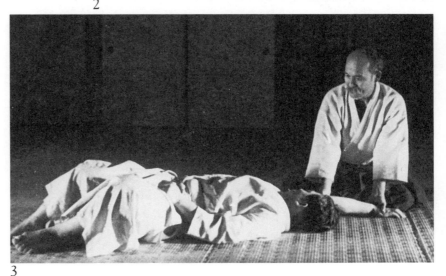

3

1

2

Kote-gaeshi variation against a collar hold (1, 2).

Good *kaiten* movements enable one to stifle a group attack. Morihei instructed his students: "Enter, turn, and blend with your opponents, front and back, right and left."

4. 呼 吸 法 *Kokyū-hō*

Kokyū-hō, "breath-power techniques," constitute the fourth pillar of
Aikidō. Morihei said, "Breath is the thread that ties creation together.
When the myriad variations of breath in the universe can be sensed, the
individual techniques of Aikidō are born." In the old days, *kokyū-hō* techniques, thought to contain the secret of true power, were never taught
publicly.

1

Morihei demonstrates the incredible
power of true *kokyū* (1), and its application in a throw (2).

2

1

2

Morihei demonstrating a *kokyū* throw as an old man (1). Following years of training in the basic *kokyū-hō* techniques, Morihei could use his breath-power to down his partners without touching them (2).

1

2

3

In basic *kokyū-hō* techniques one's partner is allowed to get a firm grip (1) in order to provide some resistance, which is then used as a gauge of one's progress in breath-power.

1

2

3

Suwari kokyū-hō, "seated breath-power training," is a basic technique practiced in every Aikidō *dōjō*, usually at the end of the training session. Morihei demonstrates the classical form (1, 2, 3, 4) and a variation with *atemi* (5, 6).

4

5

6

Suwari kokyū-hō variation shown from two different angles (2, 3).

1

Tenchi-nage variation of *suwari kokyū-hō* (1, 2).

2

3

Hand movements in *suwari kokyū-hō* shown from two different angles (3, 4).

4

1

Suwari kokyū-hō with a throw over the top. Note hand movements shown from a different angle (3).

2

3

4

1

2

Kokyū throw to the side (1, 2) and variation (3) in which the partner will be thrown to the front.

3

1

2

3

4

5

Kokyū throws against a shoulder hold. The second example (4, 5)
is a combination *kaiten* movement and *kokyū* throw.

1

2

3

4

5

Kokyū throws against a double shoulder hold (1, 2, 3) and a choke hold (4, 5).

1

2

Kokyū throws: to the inside, after entering at
a ninety-degree angle (1, 2); to the outside (3,
4); and diagonally (5, 6).

5

3

4

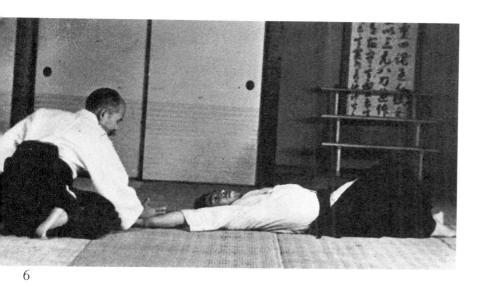

6

1

2

Kokyū throw against a double sleeve hold (1).
Note again the triangular footwork (2).

5. 押 技 *Osae-waza*

Osae-waza, "pinning techniques," make up the fifth pillar of Aikidō. Pins represent perfect control, the proper resolution of a technique. Pins also serve to stretch and stimulate a partner's muscles and joints, thus helping make them flexible, strong, and healthy.

Morihei has entered from a ninety-degree angle to apply this *ikkyō* pin.

1

2

3

4

5

The classical *ikkyō* ("pin number one") technique begins by drawing one's partner out (1), cutting down to the side (2, 3), and stepping in forcefully (4) and, from a different angle, (5). The technique finishes with a pin that immobilizes one's partner (6).

6

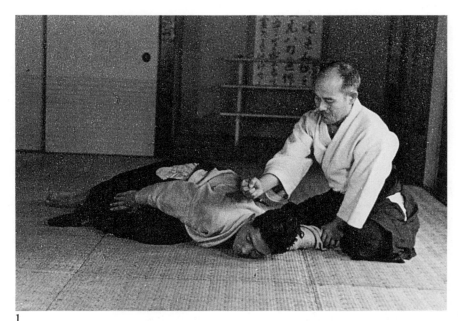

The *ikkyō* pin shown from a different angle (1) and with variations (2, 3).

3

1

2

3

4

5

Standing version of *ikkyō*. Note the correspondence with the sitting version shown overleaf.

1

2

3

4

5

Sitting version of *ikkyō*.

1

2

Ikkyō variations: to the side (1, 2); and diagonally to the front (3, 4).

3

4

1

2

Ikkyō applications against a shoulder hold: standing
(1, 2, 3); and sitting (4, 5).

3

4

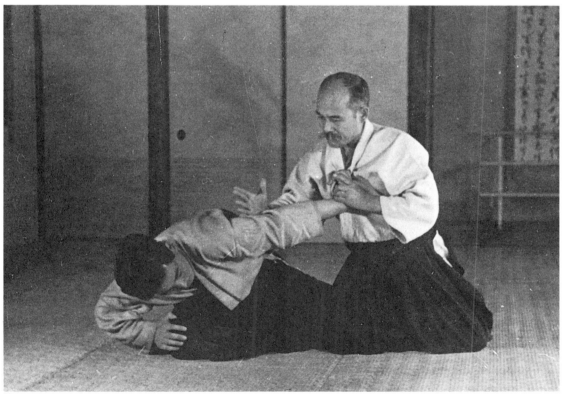

5

1

Ikkyō throw (2) or pin (3) applied against a shoulder hold.

2

3

Nikyō ("pin number two") with the concluding pin shown from two different angles (5, 6).

5

6

1

2

In this seated technique against a shoulder
hold, *nikyō* is applied twice, once at the beginning of the technique (2) and then again at
the end (6).

3

4

5

6

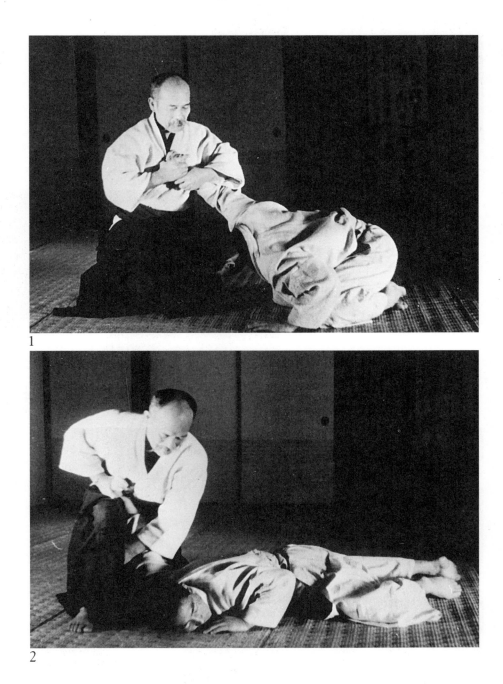

Nikyō variations against a collar hold (1, 2) and a shoulder hold (3, 4, 5).

3

4

5

1A

1B

Two more *nikyō* variations (1A, 1B, 2A, 2B) with unusual
concluding pins.

2A

2B

1

2

Sankyō ("pin number three") showing entry (1) and grip
with application of *atemi* (2).

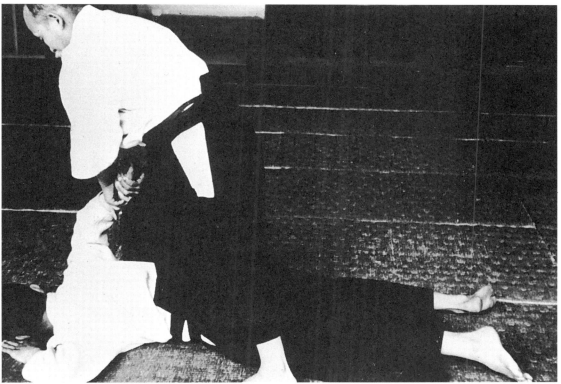

Yonkyō ("pin number four") showing proper hold (1) and pin variation (2).

The *gokyō* ("pin number five") grip.

6. 後 技 *Ushiro-waza*

Ushiro-waza, "rear techniques," are the sixth pillar of Aikidō. "Through the practice of rear techniques," Morihei wrote, "one learns how to train one's mind and body against attacks from all directions. Rear techniques open the window of one's mind and foster one's sixth sense."

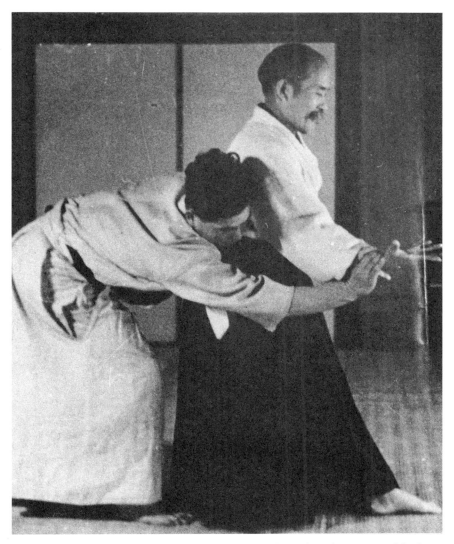

Grabbed by both hands from behind, Morihei combines breath-power and body movement to break his partner's posture.

1

2

The same attack as on the previous page is shown here from the front (1). After slipping to the side, Morihei applies an *ikkyō* pin (2).

After making a turn, Morihei throws his partner to the rear.

Morihei taught: "It is essential to train against grabs from the rear; one must train diligently to develop the enlightened ability to adapt and to turn freely to the left, right, front, or back in order to avoid and down opponents."

1

Koshi-nage, "hip throw," is very effective against attacks from the rear. Morihei demonstrates the proper positioning in (1). The complete throw is shown in (2, 3, 4).

2

3

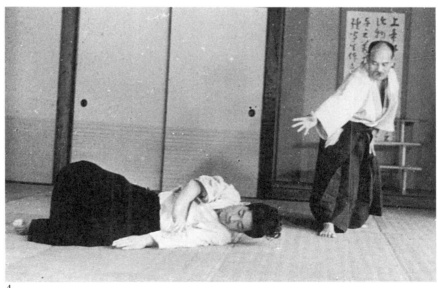

4

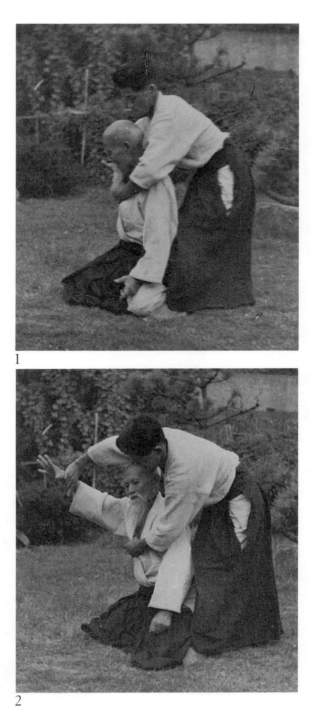

1

2

From *ushiro-muna-dori* (1), Morihei will break his partner's posture (2) and throw him to the front.

Index